Making Creative Cloth Dolls

ART DIRECTOR:
Susan McBride
PHOTOGRAPHY:
Keith & Wendy Wright
COVER DESIGN:
Barbara Zaretsky
ILLUSTRATIONS:
Orrin Lundgren
ASSISTANT EDITOR:
Veronika Alice Gunter
ASSISTANT ART DIRECTOR:
Hannes Charen
PROOFREADER:
Sherry Hames
EDITORIAL ASSISTANCE:
Rain Newcomb
EDITORIAL INTERN:
Nathalie Mornu
ART INTERN:
Shannon Yokeley

Front Cover :
Strength as interpreted by (left to right)
Tracy Stilwell, **Barbara Carleton
Evans**, **Arlinka Blair**, **Lynne Sward**, and
Pamela Hastings, 2001. Mixed media.
Photo by Keith Wright.

Back Cover:
Top right: **Barbara Carleton Evans**.
Clarity, 2001. Felt and mixed media.
Photo by Keith Wright.
Bottom left: **Margie Hennen**. *Green
Woman,* 2001. Mixed media. Photo by
Keith Wright.
Bottom right: **Pamela Hastings**. *Button-
face Dolls*, 1995. Mixed media.
Photo by Allen Bryan.

Facing Page:
Roxanne Padgett. *The Keeper*, 20 x 10
x 3 inches (50.8 x 25.4 x 7.6 cm),
1999. Sculpted face mask, fabric body,
pieced clothing, paper-box beads,
sticks, natural materials. Photo by artist

Library of Congress Cataloging-in-Publication Data

Le Van, Marthe.
  Making creative cloth dolls / Marthe Le Van.
    p. cm.
  ISBN 1-57990-334-7
    1. Dollmaking. 2. Cloth dolls. I. Title.

  TT175 .L42 2002
  745.592'21--dc21

                                                    2002020205

10 9 8 7 6 5 4 3

Published by Lark Books, a division of
Sterling Publishing Co., Inc.
387 Park Avenue South
New York, N.Y. 10016

© 2002, Lark Books

Distributed in Canada by Sterling Publishing,
c/o Canadian Manda Group, One Atlantic Ave., Suite 105
Toronto, Ontario, Canada M6K 3E7

Distributed in Australia by Capricorn Link (Australia) Pty Ltd.,
P.O. Box 704, Windsor, NSW 2756 Australia

Distributed in the U.K. by Guild of Master Craftsman Publications Ltd.,
Castle Place 166 High Street, Lewes, East Sussex, England, BN7 1XU.
Tel: (+44) 1273 477374 • Fax: (+44) 1273 478606
Email: pubs@thegmcgroup.com • Web: www.gmcpublications.com

Every effort has been made to ensure that all the information in this book is
accurate. However, due to differing conditions, tools, and individual skills,
the publisher cannot be responsible for any injuries, losses, and other damages
that may result from the use of the information in this book.

If you have questions or comments about this book, please contact:
Lark Books
67 Broadway
Asheville, North Carolina 28801
(828) 253-0467

Manufactured in China
All rights reserved
ISBN 1-57990-334-7

Making Creative Cloth Dolls

Marthe Le Van

LARK BOOKS
A Division of Sterling Publishing Co., Inc.
New York

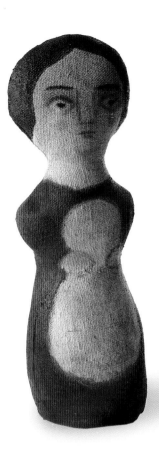

contents

introduction

If you've ever wanted to express yourself with unlimited freedom, then creating cloth dolls is the experience you've been seeking. Whether you're looking for a satisfying hobby or a new path for your artistic career, cloth dolls have plenty to offer. When you hear the term "doll," you may picture porcelain-faced maidens, ideal in proportion and dress, or children's companions, threadbare and lumpy from love. This book doesn't focus on the rosy-cheeked cherubs you may have played with as a child, but on more thought-provoking and passionate work. Today, there is a fascinating and very active assortment of contemporary artists who are producing figure-based cloth sculpture. They frequently refer to their one-of-a-kind creations as *art dolls* or *spirit dolls*. This is a vibrant global community, and its numbers are growing for good reason. I'm delighted to have the opportunity to share their work with you, and hope you'll become involved in this most rewarding craft.

Colors, textures, and patterns all woven together make textiles an irresistible artistic material. Only fabric offers such a refined visual and tactile harmony. Cloth is also an utterly comfortable material with which to begin your dollmaking journey. You're already personally connected to the feel, smell, and color of cloth. To experience this, just pause to absorb and appreciate the sensations of your favorite clothes, linens, and upholstery.

Cloth is a superb all-purpose dollmaking medium. It's readily available, and is easily sewn using basic equipment. Most fabrics are relatively inexpensive. Since doll patterns require little yardage, you can collect and reuse scrap fabrics. Cloth's flexibility lets you to be very creative. You can alter and adorn its surface, or manipulate the fabric itself to generate dimension. There's no right or wrong way to use fabric, so you're free to follow your own muse as you explore, experiment, and create.

To show just how receptive dolls are to different individual styles, we commissioned Barbara Carleton Evans to draft three simple doll patterns. The three doll forms, titled Clarity, Energy, and Strength, were created to serve as "blank canvas projects," or identical foundations for diverse interpretations. These three patterns were sent to five doll artists with the directive to make the dolls their own. Through use of the designers' technical knowledge, distinct specialties, and original visions, 15 wholly different versions were created. We've given you the basic "blank canvas" patterns so you can use your own imagination and experience to render your own Clarity, Energy, and Strength. We've also provided step-by-step instructions for the artists' dolls if you choose to follow their designs.

Many other talented artists were invited to create special dolls for this book. The variety of work we received was astounding, and it's our pleasure to share their dolls with you. Each of the dolls is beautifully photographed and accompanied by easy-to-follow instructions. For those of you who are novice sewers or are just entering the dollmaking field, Barbara Carleton Evan's Don't Call Me a Square on page 88 is a great project to start with. For those of you looking for more complex projects, you're certain to be challenged by JoAnn Pinto's Metamorphosis on page 97. In this original-pattern section, you'll find even more exciting dollmaking materials and techniques to explore. For example, in addition to standard stuffing, alternative doll supports are featured, ranging from recycled travel-size plastic bottles (see Margi Hennen's Green Woman on page 101 and Kathryn Belzer's Blessing Doll on page 104) to galvanized wire (see Beth Carter's Wily Woman on page 81).

For further insight and inspiration, we've included an extensive gallery of contemporary cloth dolls. Their makers are as diverse as the dolls themselves, and we're grateful for their participation. Many artists were kind enough to put their artistic vision into words. These statements accompany the visual images. In addition, you'll find a series of short articles, under the heading "Dolls For...," illustrating the deep cultural significance of dolls throughout history. Learning about the traditional ceremonial and social functions of dolls may motivate you to develop your own one-of-a-kind doll and sustain its heritage.

Art that's edgy really lights my fire. I favor artists who, through feats of their imagination, illuminate my eyes and mind. I was thrilled when I first discovered dolls that challenged and expanded my perception. Soon into my research, I became aware of the high number of artists working in this vein, and was drawn to their daring creations. To me, these dolls can convey profound emotional expressions and clear intellectual declarations. Often intimate personal narratives, they are always impressive meditations on the essence of form and of the spirit. Each doll reflects the character of its maker; perhaps in the posture and scale of its elements; the fabric selection or stitching style; or the immense display of creative freedom. Making dolls is a beautiful way to observe life, search for meaning, meet people, and discover yourself. Welcome.

the basics by Barbara Carleton Evans

GETTING STARTED

Like all art forms, learning to make cloth dolls starts with understanding a set of basic skills. If you've never made an art doll, everything you need to know to get started is in this book. You can learn many basic dollmaking skills just by sewing your way through the patterns. Anyone with fundamental sewing skills is ready to make a cloth doll. Familiarity with the equipment and materials involved is the initial challenge. If needed, refresh your grasp of simple hand- and machine- sewing to be able to fully use these techniques. This is a great time to experiment with different fabrics, sewing techniques, and dollmaking supplies. The most important training, however, is practice, practice, practice. In designing your doll, you'll have the opportunity to make many exciting choices. The awesome variety of fabrics, colors, textures, and stitches, coupled with the decisions you'll make regarding construction, proportion, stuffing, facial features, hair, clothing, and embellishments, may seem overwhelming at first.

However, one result of your practice and patience is an attitude adjustment that turns the profusion of materials and choices from apparent chaos to irresistible inspiration.

The loose parameters of the contemporary art doll allow you to freely express yourself without worry. Mixing media is important to these soft figures, so learn as much as you can about color and design, beading, embroidery, and all other skills that interest you. A curious spirit and an inquisitive mind will help you get the most from this book. For inspiration, why not take a class in a related field, study pictures of other artist's work, and attend exhibits that feature dolls? These activities are not only rewarding but also can be great learning tools that will benefit your dollmaking. There are many local and cyberspace doll clubs full of interesting people willing to share techniques, skills, and resources. It's nearly impossible to come away from a meeting without new ideas for your next doll.

Lynne Sward. *Voodoo Series #7, 2001*. Cloth, suede, sequins, beads. Photo by Keith Wright

MATERIALS & TOOLS

Using the appropriate tools and materials makes your doll construction flow much more smoothly. You'll already have most of the items you need in a basic craft sewing kit.

FABRIC

From cotton to crepe de chine to camel hair, the variety of modern fabrics is astounding. Creative people are drawn instinctively to the intriguing fibers, colors, and patterns of textiles. The flowing drape of a blouse, the intricate complexity of an ethnic rug, the dance of light through a window sheer, or the simple feel of a favorite pillowcase may capture your attention. Whatever your taste, there are plenty of fabrics to choose from, not only in fabric stores but also in thrift shops, flea markets, and garage sales. Sometimes when you're browsing through these secondhand sources, you'll stumble upon appealing vintage patterns that are no longer available in fabric stores.

Fabric is categorized into three groups based on the way their fibers or yarns are connected. Vertical and horizontal yarns are interlaced to form woven fabrics, such as many cottons and silks. Knitted fabrics, such as jersey, velour, and fleece, are made from interlocking looped stitches. Nonwoven fabrics, such as wool and synthetic felts, are created using techniques that don't fit into the previous two categories. Some types of fabrics have characteristics that necessitate special handling. (For example, knit fabrics generally have a significant amount of give in one or both directions.) For this reason, some of the dolls in this book have different sets of directions to accommodate different fabric selections.

It's always best to select the appropriate fabric type for your doll. No matter how appealing a textile appears, if it's too hard to work with, chances are you won't have a pleasant experience. Examine the weight, weave, and texture of a fabric to evaluate its potential. A doll's foundation fabrics should be strong enough to tolerate stitching, turning, stuffing, and the application of embellishments. Fragile fab-

Assorted fabrics, woven and nonwoven

rics often are too delicate and will tear, while thick or rigid fabrics won't turn and are difficult to sew. However, both of these examples are perfectly suited for decorative use before or after the doll is constructed. When selecting doll fabric, you also need to consider the size of the piece of cloth. Make sure you have enough fabric to accommodate the necessary pattern pieces. This is easy to do if you're buying new fabric (keeping in mind that widths do vary) but will take a little more attention if you're using remnants, secondhand material, or scraps.

VISION

"I try to work as subconsciously as possible when I design and name my art pieces. I have been interested in portraying figures interacting in both my paintings and my dolls. In this series, I wanted to show two figures interacting over a period of time. The Queen-of-the-May is a privileged lady, perhaps the artist, who, over the course of the three vignettes, goes from ignoring, to confronting, to embracing her darker self. In the course of the interaction, the Darker Self becomes more powerful, but more beautiful and more dynamic, as the Queen also becomes more powerful, dynamic, and celebratory as well. I did design and finish one set of figures at a time, a 'cathartic' experience."
Pamela Hastings

Take your time selecting the fabric for your doll. Consider not only the practicality of the cloth, but also its visual appeal, tactile qualities, and emotional character. Will these traits help you express your goal in making a doll? Pull out your possible trims and embellishments and evaluate them along with the fabric. Do these enhance the overall effect you're trying to create? Once you're decided upon fabric, remember to choose the best needle and thread for that particular fabric.

SEWING MACHINE

Dollmakers can use any sewing machine in good working order that they know well. Thoroughly read and absorb the detailed user's guide published by your machine's manufacturer. You'll learn practical information such as threading, winding bobbins, using accessories, and controlling tension. You can create original works of art on a standard sewing machine, so explore its decorative possibilities, too. One of them might be just the right technique to use on your next doll.

Use the correct sewing machine needles for your project, making sure that they are sharp and straight. The correct machine-needle size is determined by the weight of the fabric to be sewn. Usually, heavier-weight fabrics are best sewn with larger needles. Select the type of thread, generally cotton or polyester, that you prefer, making sure it suits the job and the needle. Although most often the thread size is the same for the bobbin and the needle, you may want to experiment with variations. Using different thread weights can yield fascinating effects. Give plenty of consideration to the color of the thread. Do you want the thread to match the fabric and virtually disappear, complement the fabric's tones, or stand in sharp contrast?

HAND-SEWING NEEDLES

The right type of needle makes a world of difference in the ease, appearance, and quality of your hand-stitching. Keep a variety of needles with your sewing supplies. Needles are commonly numbered according to their size—the smaller the number, the longer and thicker the needle.

All purpose hand-sewing needles, or *sharps*, have a medium length and small rounded eyes. For detailed handwork, you may want to choose a shorter needle, or a *between*, with a small rounded eye.

Dollmaking needles are sized up to 6 inches (15.2 cm) long. They are great for stringing thick parts, creating facial features, and working on soft sculpture. Ballpoint needles are for sewing knit fabrics. They have a rounded tip to go between the threads, not through them. For heavy embroidery or ribbon embroidery, a chenille needle may be your best bet. It's short and thick with a large eye and a very sharp point. Tapestry needles are mainly for embroidery, especially on loosely woven fabrics. They are short with a blunt tip and a long eye. An embroidery or crewel needle is medium length and has a long oval eye to hold numerous strands. Beading needles are very long and fine. Use them to attach beads or small pearls. Use upholstery needles on thick, tightly woven upholstery fabrics. For piercing leather, suede, and vinyl, you'll need a special leather needle, or *glover*. They are long and strong with a wedge tip. In the ever-expanding world of needles, there is even a self-threading variety good for those with reduced eyesight.

THREAD

There are three major categories of thread, based on its fiber. The first variety of thread comes from natural sources such as animals or plants. The most common animal fibers are silk, from the cocoons of the silkworm, and wool, from the fleece of sheep. Familiar plant fibers are cotton and linen. The second category covers threads that come from man-made sources. Synthetic threads offer new opportunities for different textures and effects. The final type of threads are blends of more than one fiber. They can be anything from a mix of silk and wool to blends of man-made fibers.

Threads come in a wide range of weights and colors. Some are twisted and must be used as one thread, while others are made up of several strands which can be separated and used singly or put together in different weight and color combinations. It's important to select the appropriate type of thread for the sewing technique you're using.

Clockwise from top left: thread, dollmaking needles, assorted hand-sewing needles, straight pins, thimble, embroidery thread

For decorative stitching, such as applique, embroidery, and beading, you may need or want to use a different type of thread than that used for basic hand- and machine-sewing. This opens up yet another world of exciting creative discovery.

ADHESIVES

There are many excellent fabric adhesives available, but one variety won't fit all fabrics. Use an adhesive that is appropriate for the fabric with which you're working. In general, adhesives that hold immediately and dry quickly are the most satisfactory to use. Read and follow the instructions printed on the bottle. Test all adhesive on scraps of the fabric you'll be using or on similar fabric to be sure they do the intended job. After the test samples dry thoroughly, examine them to see if the adhesives bleed through or discolor the fabric.

There are also several products on the market that help keep woven and knitted fabric edges from fraying. These are useful when you're using fabric that ravels easily, or when you're making small dolls with very narrow seam allowances. Choose the product best suited for the fabric you're using, and apply these products outside the stitching lines.

IRONS

An iron is a necessary tool for any kind of sewing. Most fabrics benefit from ironing. Non-iron fabrics are even better-looking when given a gentle press. All dollmaking fabrics should be ironed at the start of a project, and routinely as your sewing progresses. Often, fabric hems need to be pressed before sewing, making an iron nearly indispensable to the dollmaker. Follow the temperature recommendations from your iron's manufacturer, often printed on the setting dial. To prevent fabric damage from excessive heat and direct contact, iron the wrong side of the fabric if possible. You also can use a lightweight pressing cloth between the iron and fabric.

STUFFING

With dolls, much as with people, what's inside is just as important as what's outside. Polyester rates as the most popular stuffing, but people use all sorts of materials: horsehair, newspaper, straw, sawdust, dried beans, cotton and wool, macaroni noodles, shredded foam, sand, feathers, old rags, and dried aromatic herbs are just a few examples. Polyester fiber's advantages over other substances are numerous: it handles easily; is resilient (springs back after crushing); packs well to create a firm, evenly filled doll; weighs next to nothing; washes well and dries quickly; costs little; and is easy to find. High-loft varieties of polyester filling are more effective than cheaper grades, which tend to be thin and dense, and can compact down into lumps. Although other materials may work for a particular doll, they

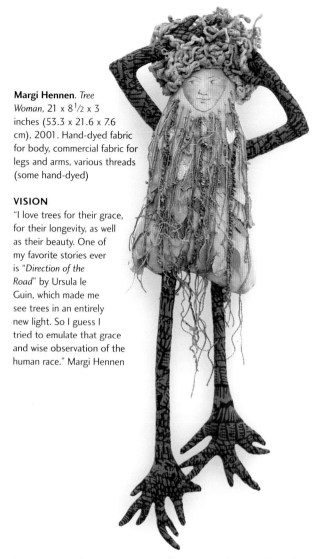

Margi Hennen. *Tree Woman*, 21 x 8 1/2 x 3 inches (53.3 x 21.6 x 7.6 cm), 2001. Hand-dyed fabric for body, commercial fabric for legs and arms, various threads (some hand-dyed)

VISION

"I love trees for their grace, for their longevity, as well as their beauty. One of my favorite stories ever is *"Direction of the Road"* by Ursula le Guin, which made me see trees in an entirely new light. So I guess I tried to emulate that grace and wise observation of the human race." Margi Hennen

have certain disadvantages, so choose carefully. Rubber foam deteriorates with wear. Wool attracts moths. Certain dried-plant materials must stay dry. Beans and seeds shift a lot inside the doll body. Noodles won't stand up to crushing. Finally, sawdust and sand add a lot of weight.

It takes practice to develop good stuffing skills. Well-designed and well-executed stuffing has considerable bearing on the overall effect of the doll, so take your time and give this task the patient attention it deserves. Different art dolls require different stuffing styles. Some are firm to the point of rigidity, while others derive a lot of character because they are slack or asymmetrical. You may need to use two or three different kinds of filler in a doll to achieve the effect you want. Your stuffing style also may be influenced by how you plan to embellish your doll. For instance, a firmly stuffed doll is easier to heavily bead.

STUFFING TIPS

Stuffing techniques vary from person to person, but here are a few standard practices:

- Always work in the direction of the unstitched opening.

- Make sure the amount of stuffing you use at one time fits the area being stuffed.

- Try not to force too much filling into too small a space. This can result in awkward, lumpy shapes and stressed seams.

- Stuff the smallest sections of the piece you're working on prior to moving on to the larger areas. For example, it's wise to fill the fingers and toes before the hands and feet.

- When stuffing larger cavities, such as torsos, gradually work from the outside edges to the center of the form.

- To stuff narrow shapes such as hands with fingers, begin to stuff them before you turn the fabric right side out. Start by turning out and filling the fingers, then turn out the hand and fill it, and finally do the arm.

- To adjust stuffing that's already inside a doll, use a long needle to shift its filling.

STUFFING TOOLS

To get the best results, you have to push the right amount of stuffing precisely into place. Many shapes stuff well by hand, but small, slender shapes like fingers or legs require a long narrow tool to push the filler all the way to the end. It's important to choose the right tool to fit the area you're stuffing. Simple objects you may already have around the house will often do the trick, or you can buy commercial stuffing tools. You can use dowels of varying widths, chopsticks, hemostats, and bamboo skewers to place small amounts of stuffing into hard-to-reach spots. (*Hemostats*, which look like scissors with tweezer tips, are sometimes called *locking forceps* or *needle drivers*.) You also can use a large knitting needle, a paintbrush handle, or an unsharpened pencil. Place or wrap a small wad of fiber on the tip of your tool, then insert that into the opening, and push the wad to the bottom. The stuffing material should stay in place when the tool is removed.

Top to bottom: stuffing tool, polyester fiber stuffing, turning tools

BASIC SEWING KIT

You probably already know about and have many of the supplies you'll need to make the projects in this book, but it's always good to be reminded of the basics. This list of fundamentals is designed to make your dollmaking experience more fulfilling and shorten each project's supply list. If you don't have to stop to search for a pencil or tape measure, you'll really be able to let the creative juices flow!

FOR MEASURING
Tape measure

Short ruler

Yardstick

FOR MARKING
Soft lead pencil

Erasable marking pen

Tailor's chalk

Fine-point marking pen

Heavyweight paper, cardboard, or poster board

FOR CUTTING
Utility scissors

Fabric shears

Embroidery scissors

Pinking shears

FOR PRESSING
Steam iron

Ironing board

Press cloth

FOR SEWING
Hand-sewing needles

Sewing thread in a variety of colors

Needle threaders, optional

Thimble

Straight pins

Pincushion or pin holder

Safety pins

Seam sealant (fray retardant)

FOR STUFFING
Good quality polyester or alternate material

Stuffing tool

FOR NOTES & INSPIRATION
Notebook or journal

Tape or glue

Colored pencils, markers, or crayons

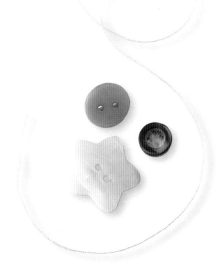

TECHNIQUES

Whether you're an experienced or occasional sewer, you may want to
brush up on the basics before beginning cloth doll projects.
The following sections present technical information relevant to the
projects in this book, as well as practical tips.

PATTERN MARKINGS

When you're making a doll from a pattern, certain guidelines need to be followed. To make your transfer, cutting, and sewing more accurate, a shorthand system of symbols are marked on the patterns to indicate what actions to take. If you haven't sewn recently from a pattern, use the table below as a reference.

CUTTING LINE

Cut on top of or just inside this line.

SEWING LINE

Sew the seams directly on this line.

SEAM ALLOWANCE

The area between the cutting line and the sewing line. Use a 1/4-inch (6 mm) seam allowance unless otherwise directed.

GUIDE LINE

Marks the location for actions such as basting, topstitching, gathering, and hair placement.

MATCH POINTS

A B C ● ● ●

Symbols that clarify sewing sequence. Often letters or bullets.

CENTER FRONT

CF

CENTER BACK

CB

CLIP

\ | /

Clip the seam allowance to release the strain, especially on curves (see figure 1).

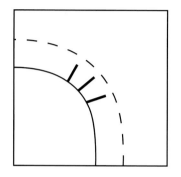

Figure 1

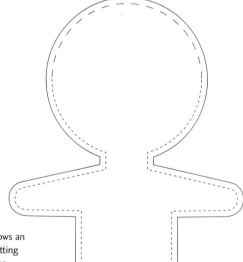

This pattern shows an example of a cutting line, a sewing line, and a guide line.

MAKING PATTERN TEMPLATES

Each of this book's patterns must be photocopied according to the project notes. You can turn your paper copies into sturdier templates by gluing the paper to thin cardboard or poster board, and cutting them out once the glue is completely dry. To transfer the shapes to the fabric, trace around the sturdy templates with a soft pencil, dressmaker's chalk, or erasable marking pen. Always trace onto the back, or *wrong* side of the fabric, unless directed otherwise (the front is called the *right* side). When you're working with thin fabric, you can fold the right sides of the fabric together and lay out just one template for each facing piece. Remember to transfer all the pattern markings.

FUNCTIONAL HAND−STITCHES

Several stitches frequently used in hand sewing are illustrated in figure 2. The running stitch works well for basting and gathering; the backstitch and ladder stitch make great seams; and overcasting is the best way to whipstitch fabric edges together. A stab stitch is a good choice when you're sewing on the right side of the fabric, or topstitching.

Figure 2

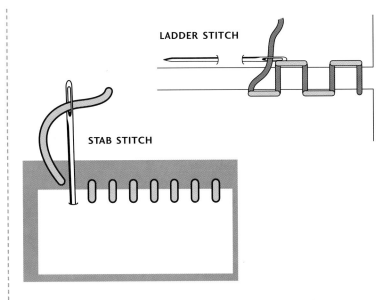

LADDER STITCH

STAB STITCH

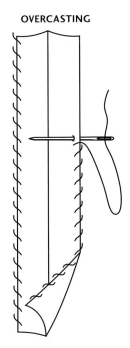

OVERCASTING

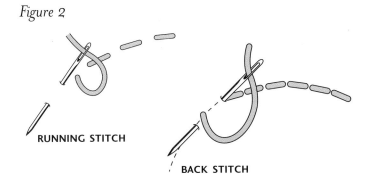

RUNNING STITCH

BACK STITCH

DECORATIVE HAND-STITCHES

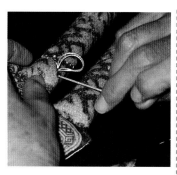

Classic embroidery stitches have many uses on cloth dolls, such as creating facial features, highlighting pattern details, adding texture to fabric, and securing appliques in a unique way. The most popular embroidery stitches are illustrated in figure 3. Cotton floss is the most commonly used thread. Floss comes in many weights and colors, and its individual strands can be separated to suit your needs. The most frequently used stitches are the stem stitch for outlines, the satin stitch for solid color blocks, French knots for dots and texture, and straight stitches for expressive lines and securing appliques. There are many more decorative stitches you can apply to great effect. Consult embroidery books or even look on the Internet to find hundreds of examples.

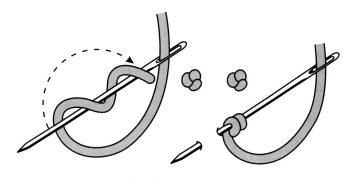

FRENCH KNOTS

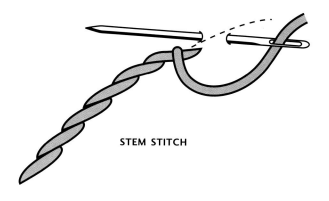

STEM STITCH

Figure 3

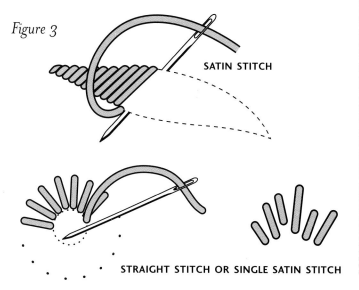

SATIN STITCH

STRAIGHT STITCH OR SINGLE SATIN STITCH

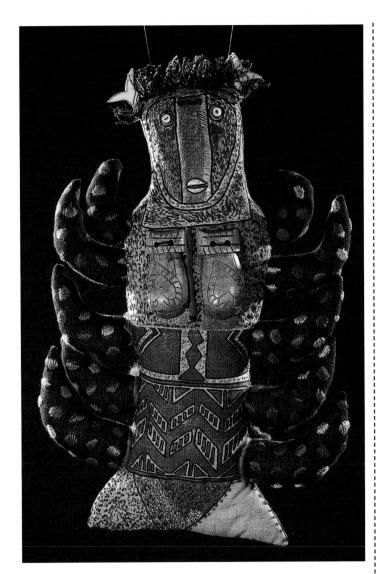

Arlinka Blair. *Coming Into Wisdom,* 16 x 10 inches (40.6 x 25.4 cm), 2001. Linoleum-block printing, heavy decorative stitching and embroidery; vintage wooden castanets, Turkish printed cotton, cowrie shell. Photo by Jonathan Blair

VISION

"This doll was inspired by the found object castanets and evolved from my imagination and exploration of body shapes and forms. I like to create non-conventional shapes that suggest arms but actually are not. To me, this figure represents a sort of 'Goddess' image, and the idea of wisdom was also conveyed." Arlinka Blair

DECORATION

The word *embellish* means to make beautiful, as well as to decorate, improve, adorn, or make more ornate. It also means to exaggerate, and nothing is more fun than going over the top when embellishing dolls. There's no limit to materials and ideas. You can use the old standbys such as lace, beads, buttons, trims, and ribbons, or go crazy with bottle caps, scraps of fake fur, pieces of tumbled glass, shells, or feathers.

Everywhere you go, keep an eye out for interesting materials or embellishments. Stay receptive to the unusual: in the dollhouse accessories' or party favors' section of a crafts store, you might find tiny treasures to adorn your doll; or, while shopping for fake plants for your aquarium, you might discover interesting doll "hair". You can get great fabrics and costume jewelry for a steal at garage sales, and interesting fibers can be found at fishing stores. Once you start looking through a dollmaker's eyes, you'll find raw materials everywhere. Any object or fabric that can be sewn to, hung on, wrapped around, or stuffed inside a doll has potential. If you look for items with interesting shapes, colors, and textures, without considering their intended use, you'll find a new world of possibilities. Beyond the usual buttons, baubles, and beads, your doll designs can benefit greatly from such varied decorations as hardware, leaves and twigs, rubber bands, scrap metal, fishing tackle, and much more. In Strength by Arlinka Blair on page 74, you'll note a rusty bottle cap used for a mouth. With her keen eye, she turned recycled trash into an expression to treasure.

Various trims

If you scavenge something particularly intriguing, why not build a whole doll around it? This is a great exercise to show just how meaningful dollmaking can be. You have made a personal connection with an object and now have the opportunity to make it part of your art. Think (and look) twice before throwing away rubbish or making a donation to the thrift store, and make sure you're alerted when friends and relatives are cleaning. Some of their odds and ends may find a cherished spot in your cloth or trim stash. Look at the materials you've stored to "make a special doll with some day." Do you remember why they appealed to you? Do they still have meaning? If so, why not make *today* the day you start that special doll?

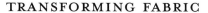

TRANSFORMING FABRIC

Modifying fabrics is one of the most enjoyable ways to personalize your doll. Numerous products, such as fabric paints and dyes, can be applied in many different ways, allowing almost any type of fabric to be colored. These opportunities allow you to create unique fabrics, rather than rely on the prints and colors your local retailer supplies. You also can use other craft techniques, including stamping, sponging, printing, and marbling, to alter fabric with great success.

Anne Mayer Hesse. *Hoop Dancer*, 24 x 14 x 8 inches (60.9 x 35.6 x 20.3 cm), 2000. Cloth over wood and wire armature, hand-beaded face, yarn-wrapped wire to form hoop; exotic yarns, variety of fabrics, paint, beads. Photo by Jerry Anthony

VISION
"Hoop Dancer reflects one aspect of woman—how so many of us 'make our own hoops' and then have to dance through them...!" Anne Mayer Hesse

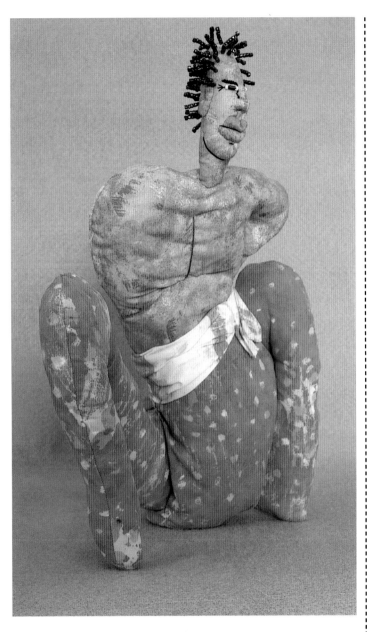

Kathryn Belzer. *When Leila Heard That Bernie Would Be There, She Was Drawn as a Moth to the Class Reunion (back)*, 18 inches (45.7 cm), 2000. Cloth over foam. Photo by Dan Abriel

Deb Shattil. *Man of the Earth*, 10$^1/_2$ x 7$^1/_2$ x 5 inches (26.7 x 19 x 12.7 cm), 2001. Fabric (some hand-painted), beaded hair; body is articulated with topstitching; interior wire armature. Photo by artist

VISION
"Sometimes I leave out body parts in favor of a nice silhouette. I describe the figure with shapes instead of anatomy."
Deb Shattil

FABRIC PAINTS

Water-based fabric paint is the easiest variety to use and its colors are permanent. Linen, rayon, cotton, silk, and wool can be colored with water-based paint. The paint lies on the surface of the fabric and is heat-set with an iron or clothes dryer. When considering a fabric paint, look carefully at its label for intended use. Some fabric paints yield beautiful effects, but their transparent colors can be appreciated only on light fabrics. Dark-colored fabrics require opaque fabric paints. There's no limit to the way you can apply fabric paints. They can be brushed, splattered, or sprayed, all to great effect.

Many different fabric paints are suitable for printing. All you have to do is put the paint on the stamp or block, and then press it against the fabric. Printing with sponges, stenciling, and screen printing are other excellent ways to add design to your fabric.

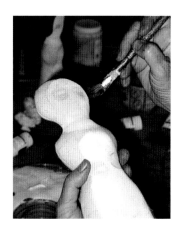

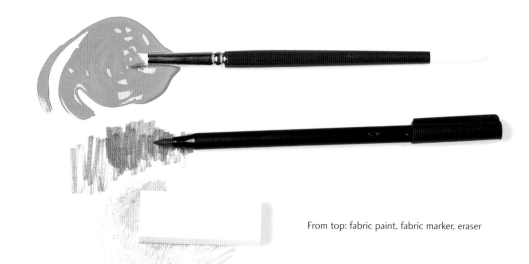

From top: fabric paint, fabric marker, eraser

FABRIC MARKERS

Fabric markers come in an astonishing array of colors. Using a fine-, medium-, or wide-tip marker, you can draw images, lines or words, or add shading or detail to a design. Other kinds of pens can be used to decorate your doll, as long as they're described as indelible on fabric.

FABRIC DYES

Chances are you've already experimented with dyeing fabric. Whether you tie-dyed a t-shirt or stone-washed a pair of jeans, you've seen how quick and easy it is to dramatically transform the appearance of fabric. You can dye fabric through direct application techniques (paint, drip, sprinkle, spray, discharge), immersion, or a combination of both. The advantage of working with dyes rather than paints is that they don't change the *hand* of the fabric (the way the fabric feels when touched). Even high-quality textile paint sits on the surface of the fabric, making it stiffer and heavier. Dyes, however, chemically react with the fibers to become part of the fabric and leave it as soft as it was originally.

Start by choosing the right type of fabric to dye. Natural fabrics are generally preferable to man-made. To obtain the best results, read and closely follow the dye manufacturer's directions regarding procedure and safety. Your fabric-dyeing skills will build with practice. There are many fabric dyers who are happy to share their practices and tips either in classes, publications, or on the Internet. Dyeing your own fabrics is a fabulous skill to use in conjunction with making dolls.

FABRIC TRANSFERS

You can transfer photocopied images onto fabric in several ways, bearing in mind that the appearance of the transfer varies depending on the process used. Keep in mind that most transfer methods reverse the image (and any words) onto the fabric. If you wish to prevent this, use a "mirror-image" photocopy.

CHEMICAL AGENTS

Solvent transfers, in the form of various liquids and pastes, are inexpensive and easy. Photo-transfer medium, acetone, liquid solvent, and paint stripper all work effectively. For most solvents, you simply make a photocopy of the image, coat the copy with the chemical agent, place the coated photocopy on the fabric, and use a brayer or even an old spoon to rub the image onto the fabric. You must heat-set the image by ironing the reverse side of the fabric after the transfer dries completely.

PHOTO−TRANSFER SHEETS

These versatile sheets of specially treated paper produce a high quality transfer. In a two-part process, you first impose the image onto the transfer sheet, and then move it onto the fabric. Most full-service copy shops will do either or both of these steps for you, or you can do it yourself.

The most common method of getting an image onto the transfer sheet is via a photocopier. The coated sheets fit nicely into the copier's paper drawer. Alternatively, if you have a computer, a printer, and a way of importing digitized images into your computer, you can print directly onto the transfer sheets. Many printer and photocopier manufacturers make transfer sheets specifically for their equipment, so buy accordingly and follow their instructions. (To save money, try to get as many images as possible onto a sheet of transfer paper and cut

Lesley Riley. *Healing Heart*,
25 x 19 x 5 1/2 inches (63.5 x 48.3 x
14 cm), 2001. Canvas, dye-painted
with acrylic inks, patinated copper
paints, computer-image transfer, mohair,
wood. Photo by PRS Associates

VISION
"There is no greater joy than having
others find themselves in my art."
Lesley Riley

them apart for later use.) Once you have the image on the transfer sheet, heat-transfer it to the fabric with an iron.

OTHER TRANSFER TECHNIQUES

There are other options to play with as well. You could have a rubber stamp made from a favorite photo or design. And an ingenious "blueprint" fabric receives an image when it's exposed to the sun. Certain silk fabrics even can be run through a computer printer.

RUBBER STAMPING

Here are just a few of the fabulous ways you can combine stamping with art dolls: cover the fabric with images, words, sayings, and quotes; use stamps as embroidery patterns; emboss velvet; stamp with bleach on dark fabric; stamp shrink plastic and shrink it for jewelry, hair, or charms; make books, cards, or signs for your doll to hold; stamp decorative designs on the doll's environment or display; make impressions in paper, polymer clay, hot embossing powder, warm sealing wax, or hot glue for doll components. There are many rubber stamping books, magazines, and Web sites that explain in detail how to do each of the above techniques.

You can purchase pre-cut fabric stamps or make your own, but keep in mind that fabric stamps are different from paper stamps. Fabric stamps are cut deeper to avoid loosing detail. You need deeply cut stamps when stamping particularly soft and pliable fabrics and for embossing velvet.

BEADING

Beading is one of many needlework skills that can be used to add extra pizzazz to your dolls. Beads add dimension, sparkle, and richness, whether they are used sparingly as part of the embellishment, or as a major component of the doll. Some beaded dolls are fabric forms encrusted with sewn-on beads, while others are designed using one of the beadweaving techniques that constructs hollow forms. Many traditional bead-fringing techniques make excellent hair for small dolls.

When sewing beads onto dolls, it's important to firmly anchor the thread at the start, the finish, and numerous points in between. Beading needles are different from regular sewing needles: they have slim eyes, are thinner, and come in several sizes and types. Beading thread also comes in several sizes, many colors, and is much stronger than thread made for sewing fabric. Your local bead or craft store can help you choose the appropriate supplies for the beads you plan to use on your doll.

Patti Medaris Culea. *Jubilant Juliette* (detail), 2001. Photo by Keith Wright

A variety of beads and buttons

22

Megan Noël. *Angel Doll*, 8¼ x 7¼ x 2¼ inches (20.9 x 18.4 x 5.7 cm), 2000. Bead embroidery on synthetic suede; seed beads, glass beads, ammonite fossil, silver charm. Photo by Theresa Batty

Details of front and back of doll

23

FORMING A PERSONALITY

Defining your doll's character is a significant part of the design process. Sometimes, during the act of creation, the doll's personality is immediately obvious, while other dolls take more time to reveal their identity.

CREATING FACES

There are many different approaches to making doll faces. They can be hand- or machine-embroidered; drawn or painted; consist of sewn-on objects that represent features; beaded, appliquéd, or needle-sculpted; transferred with any one of a number of techniques; or created by using a combination of these methods. Abstract dolls often have no faces at all, just a shape that suggests a face. Many commercial illustrators draw marvelously expressive yet simple faces, as do some children's book illustrators. If you find making faces to be a challenging task, or are looking for new inspirations, a trip to your local library might be a great help.

Arlinka Blair. *Outsider*, 7 x 3 inches (17.8 x 7.6 cm), 1999. Indian head nickel, string, fibers, thread, cotton cloth, ribbon, vintage buttons, rayon fringed strips. Photo by Jonathan Blair

VISION

"This doll is from a series I did of very small forms. I wanted to explore wrapping and binding and keeping the figure simple and primitive. I love the way the 'eyes' convey a look of both innocence and madness. This doll also reflects an interest in outsider art and mental illness." Arlinka Blair

CONSTRUCTING HAIR

What you use for hair depends upon the type of doll you're creating. There are many kinds of hair made especially for dollmakers that are available wherever doll supplies are sold. Most of these try to look like real hair and are particularly well-suited for realistic dolls. Natural fibers, such as some very long staple fleeces, flax, and human hair, also can be used. Pieces from wigs that have been taken apart also work.

If you're making abstract dolls, anything goes, and the "hair" is as likely to come from the workshop, craft room, woods, seashore, or recycling bin as it is from a store. As you study the dolls in this book you'll see some of the possibilities. Other ideas for doll hair will occur to you as you continue to create dolls. A few of the possibilities are: wire corkscrew curls; metal, plastic, and shrink-plastic charms; beads; small interesting metal parts from the hardware store; tiny pinecones, seedpods, and seashells; wire-wrapped sea glass; ribbons and yarn; feathers; fiber; painted-on hair; head wraps instead of hair; embroidery and decorative threads; corn husks and dried corn silk; stuffed fabric shapes; gathered lace, rickrack, and other trims; fringes of all kinds; fur; palmetto fiber; ribbon roses; artificial flowers; buttons; handmade felt "worms;" and limitless other materials.

Beth Carter. *Wily Woman* (detail), 2001. Mixed Media.

ASSEMBLING THE DOLL

When making found-object dolls, or using very dissimilar materials to construct a doll, you need to figure out how to hold it all together. This usually means that a variety of methods will be used. Parts may be wired, glued, or sewn together, or they may be tied on. A drill is very helpful in making holes so objects can be securely fastened together. If you want to use an object which does not have any apparent means of attachment, wrapping part of it with wire, thread, ribbon, or other fibers will give you a way to fasten it onto the doll. Some experimentation, outside-the-box thinking, and really good glue usually will enable you to fasten that great little metal/glass/plastic object to the doll.

Roxanne Padgett. *Wise Woman*, 17 x 13 x 6 inches (43.2 x 33 x 15.2 cm), 1999. Sculpted face mask, hand-sewn fabric; daisy root, beads, strings, sticks, roots. Photo by Isaac Bailey

VISION
"Exploring the human form with the use of natural materials."
Roxanne Padgett

DESIGNING YOUR OWN DOLL

Art dolls are as varied as their makers, and reveal a vigorous creative spirit at work. When designing your own doll, it may help to explore methods for tapping your creativity. With practice, you'll learn to take risks and trust your vision, embracing change as it occurs.

JOURNALING

Keeping a journal specific to your doll-making pursuits is not only a satisfying creative expression but can suit your individual needs. Journals can expand beyond text to incorporate sketches and collage. Emotions, memories, and messages can be expressed meaningfully by combining words with pattern and color, and much insight can spring from these simple beginnings. Keeping a record of interesting lines and

Figure studies on a bulletin board in Pamela Hastings' studio

colors can serve as a wellspring of inspiration. Noting the varying success of your trials and errors serves as a reminder for future projects. A journal also can help you perceive and develop your

Above and below: figure studies on the journal pages of Arlinka Blair

inner vision in new and exciting ways.

Keep a sketchbook and a pencil with you at all times. While strolling through the grocery store, you may see something that kindles your creative spirit, but later, you may forget it. Write it down. These journal entries can serve to jog your memory. You don't have to draw like Leonardo da Vinci to jot down ideas and make little sketches that you can use for inspiration when you design a doll.

CONCEPTUALIZING

Since art dolls emphasize image and idea over function, these matters become the center of a doll's design. In the doll-planning stages, it's important to think about conceptual issues, such as the impact of shape. Do shapes have meaning for you as an artist, and what shape will the doll take? A good example of shape holding meaning is the heart—the universal symbol for love. If the heart means love, then what association do you hold for other forms, such as circles, squares, triangles, or rectangles? Try sketching some of these shapes onto paper, in varying proportions, and write down the words that come to mind. Invent original doll shapes by cutting out different forms and moving them around. A doll with a square head, triangle body, and circle hands and feet will do wonders to free your mind from the pressures of realism. Think about who the doll is meant for—perhaps a friend who needs comfort and encouragement. Is the doll being made to commemorate an important event in your own life? Some forms can sooth, while others excite. Shapes carry emotion, and you can design your doll to convey a specific feeling. Clarity, Energy, and Strength, the Blank Canvas Projects on page 29, are all examples of dolls with spirit.

Once the shape of the doll is set, its size must be determined. If you're using the doll as a sampler to try out a new technique, you might want a larger surface area. Stamping and painting may need more room than beading and wrapping, so take your intended methods into consideration. What life do you envision for the doll? Will it be stationary or travel, displayed as a mantel showpiece, or given as a special gift of courage?

Gabe Cyr. *Keepers of a Single Heart*, 37 x 14 x 2 inches (93.9 x 35.6 x 5 cm), 2000. Sewn and stuffed single-piece shoulders and yoke, hand-dyed, beaded, and embroidered raw silk yoke; arms wrapped on wire armature, painted and beaded head, hand-felted, and embellished heart; fabric strips, ribbons, beads, additional stuffed elements. Photo by Richard Babb

VISION
"The media I've explored over the past 30 years as an artist all find their way into my figure work—and half of the found objects I've tripped across too!" Gabe Cyr

26

PROPORTION

Realistic art dolls are proportioned exactly like real people. The artists who create them study anatomy and understand the interplay of bone, muscles, and tissue as positions and expressions change. Abstract art doll forms, made to represent an idea, rather than a real person, may have deliberately elongated, truncated, or nonexistent body parts to further emphasize the point the designer intended to make. An abstract art doll is a sculpture. Its components, however strange, should be designed to work in harmony with each other.

MOVEMENT

Dolls with joints are designed to move, and can be placed in many different positions. Skill in making several kinds of joints allows you to make wonderfully articulated dolls. However, even a flat "pancake" doll can be given the appearance of movement by designing it so that arms and legs are bent into running, jumping, or dancing positions. Looking at books and photos of basic ballet poses or bodies in motion will give you ideas for doll shapes that suggest movement.

Deborah C. Pope. *The Eggman*, 11 1/2 x 9 x 7 inches (29.2 x 22.9 x 17.8 cm), 2001. Merino wool with wire armature, polymer clay; hand-felted in the traditional hot-water-and-soap technique, sculpted before and after felting with felting needles. Photo by artist

VISION

"When some colleagues saw *The Eggman* for the first time, they wondered if I'd saved my children's baby teeth to make his. No, they are polymer clay!" Deborah C. Pope

Dee Dee Triplett. *Jacks in the Pulpit*, 24 x 10 x 8 inches (60.9 x 25.4 x 20.3 cm), 1998. Fabric, wood base. Photo by Evan Bracken

VISION

"I believe wildflowers play in the woods when we aren't looking...this piece is a symphony in color play: red-violet and yellow green." Dee Dee Triplett

THE WILLFUL DOLL

A funny thing happens when you make a cloth doll. As you stitch and stuff, your doll's personality begins to emerge, sometimes leading you in a different direction from what you originally planned. You may have dreamed of sweet pink ruffles and lace, but your doll insists on a glitzy red dress and marabou feathers pinned into her elegant hairdo. Resist the impulse to force the doll to bend to your will. No amount of coaxing will get the doll back into those pink ruffles, so you might as well put them away and get out the box of glamour fabrics and trims. At this point, it's a good idea to take a break and focus your attention elsewhere for a while. Coming back to your doll with fresh eyes often can produce new insights and inspiration. Watching a doll change from what you thought you were making into an entirely different personality is one of the fascinations of cloth dollmaking. It's a little bit like helping a child grow up to be the person she wants to be, rather than the person you had imagined her to be. Use this willfulness of the doll as a creative opportunity to explore new ideas. Listen to your instincts and play with the possibilities. Enjoy the creativity of the process of making a doll, and leave some room for improvisation as you go along. Being flexible and paying attention to your creative voice has its rewards. You'll have a more satisfying experience as an artist, and your dolls will be more sincere as they reflect the genuine spirit of their creator.

DISPLAYING THE DOLL

Your doll has taken many hours of your time and creative effort to finish. Now you want to show her off. Some dolls stand up by themselves. Others are planned with a wood dowel or wire that fits onto a base or a hanger. Another option is to design the doll and its display stand as an integrated whole. The woods elf can be perched on a fallen log, or the queen can have a sumptuous throne from which she reigns. Designing your doll's surrounding can be as much fun as designing the doll itself. Try not to get so carried away that the setting overwhelms the doll. Before you start a doll decide how it will be displayed, and make the stand an integral part of designing the doll.

Akiko Anzai. *Children of Neptune,* 24 inches (60.9 cm), 2001. Cloth doll stuffed with cotton, sculpted paperclay face and feet covered with fabric, decorated with silk gauze and polyester. Photo by artist

VISION
"I want to be free from any rules to make free styles of dolls. Many classic and contemporary paintings and sculptures inspire me. I'm searching into what fabrics can do to make three-dimensional forms." Akiko Anzai

BLANK CANVAS PROJECTS

For this book I created three very different "blank canvas" doll patterns. These are for you to play with and interpret in your own way by using the simple shapes as a starting point from which to begin your dollmaking adventure. I gave these same patterns to four other doll artists, each of whom is celebrated for her originality and the way she applies different skills. In their hands, these basic patterns were realized in diverse ways. Instructions for making the embellished and altered dolls are includ-ed. You're invited to follow the lead of the doll designers, trying out their techniques while developing your own creativity, building your skills, and adding your individuality into the wonderful mix.

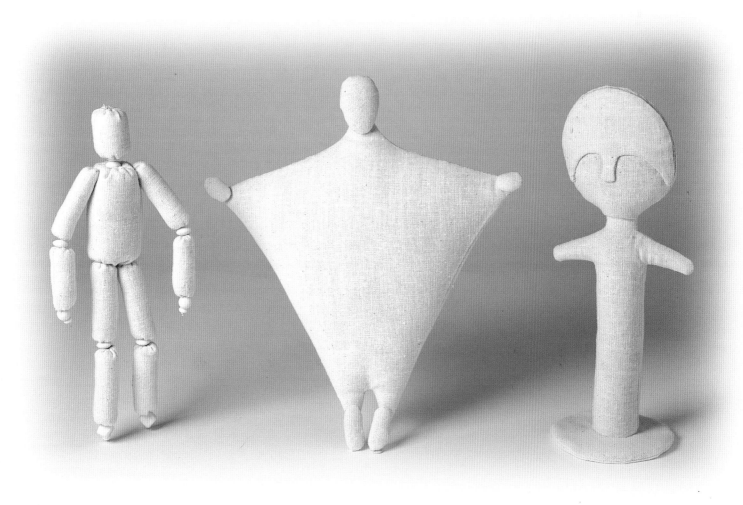

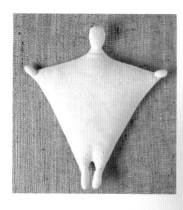

CLARITY

This doll has plenty of wide open space, so your imagination can run wild. You can use this pattern to display fantastic fabrics, whole or pieced, or experiment with many different surface decoration techniques. Clarity is perfect for rubber stamping, embroidery, painting, beading, or any other means of self-expression. Keep in mind, however, that it may be easier for you to apply your surface decorations before sewing the fabric. I recommend making this doll from nonwoven materials such as felt or suede or from a tightly woven fabric. There are alternate instructions for using woven fabrics.

ENERGY

This small doll is made by stringing together sewn and stuffed fabric body beads. Use any fabric you wish to construct Energy, as long as it's flexible enough to gather at the ends. Energy is the only "blank canvas" doll I made with joints, and they're very simple. Buttons and beads become joints when they're strung between the stuffed fabric body beads. This allows the doll's limbs to move in an animated fashion. If you find more interesting joint materials, feel free to use them. Similarly, other objects could replace some of the stuffed fabric body bead parts, such as long beads for lower arms and legs. Like all the "blank canvas" dolls, I developed this pattern with transformation in mind.

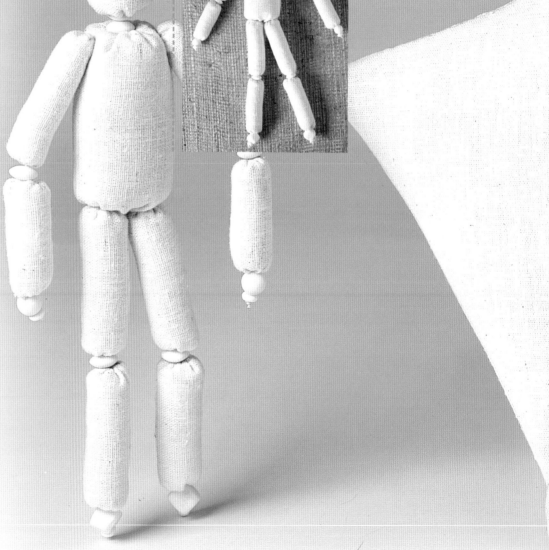

STRENGTH

Strength is a simplified fabric version of a traditional African doll originally carved from wood. The basic pattern is for woven fabrics, such as cotton, with alternate directions if you prefer to use nonwoven fabrics, such as felt. With its prominent head shape and long tubular body, Strength is equipped for all kinds of embellishments, from beading to wrapping to embroidery and more. This timeless pattern is very versatile. You can symbolize ancient traditions or construct futuristic spirits on the same fundamental figure. This is the only free-standing "blank canvas" doll I created, and there are several ways to achieve its position. Look at the instructions supplied by each designer for alternate solutions.

31

Basic Pattern for
CLARITY

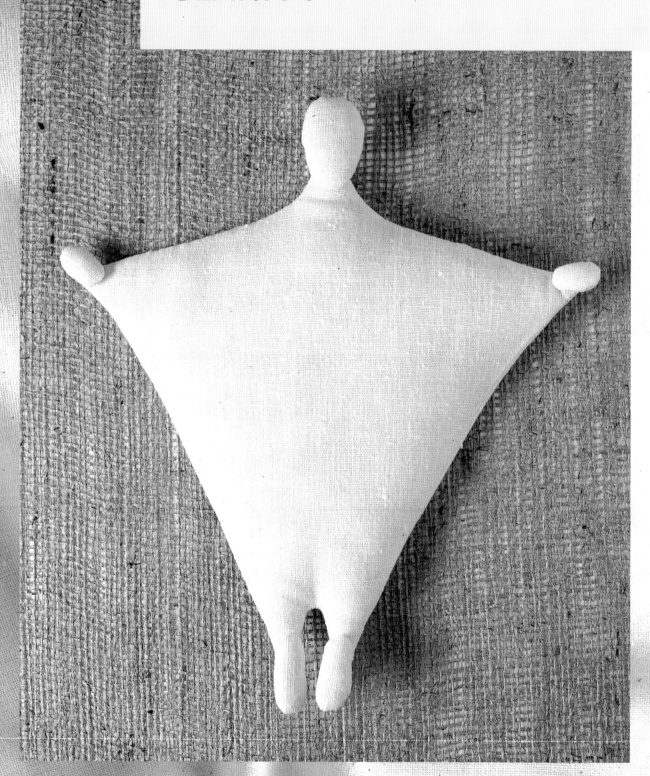

FOR WOVEN FABRIC

PREPARING THE FABRIC

1. Cut out the photocopied pattern. Place the body pattern on a double layer of fabric, right sides together. Pin the pattern in place. Trace the pattern with a soft lead pencil or a disappearing fabric marker.

ASSEMBLING THE DOLL

2. Remove the pattern and baste together the fabric layers.

3. Sew on the line from the hand, around the bottom of the doll, to the opposite hand, backstitching at the beginning and the end. Leave the doll open across the top. Trim the seam to $\frac{1}{8}$ inch (3 mm) from the stitched line. Trim the fabric to $\frac{1}{2}$ inch (1.3 cm) from the open top. Use seam sealant on the top opening if needed.

4. Finger-press a hem in the top opening so it folds exactly on the line. Pin the hem in place, and then baste. Put the basting thread knot on the right side of the fabric.

5. Clip the corners and the curves, remove the basting stitches, then turn the fabric right side out. Insert the cardboard armature into the body.

STUFFING & FINISHING THE DOLL

6. Gently stuff between the front body piece and the cardboard armature. The doll should be approximately $\frac{3}{4}$ inch (1.9 cm) thick at the center. Pin the top edges together, and then sew them closed with a ladder stitch. Remove the basting stitches.

CREATING THE HEAD HANDS, & FEET

7. Place the head pattern on doubled fabric, right sides together, trace, and then remove the pattern.

8. Machine stitch on the line, all the way around the head. Cut out the head leaving a $\frac{1}{8}$-inch (3 mm) seam allowance. Make a slit in one side of the fabric, and turn the head through this opening. Smooth out the seams, and then stuff the head. Close the slit with a ladder stitch.

9. Slip stitch the head to the doll body, making sure the slit is against and hidden by the body.

10. Repeat steps 7, 8, and 9 to create and attach the hands and feet.

FOR NONWOVEN FABRIC

PREPARING THE FABRIC & ARMATURE

1. Cut out all the body pattern pieces, and baste them to a double thickness of nonwoven fabric. Cut out the fabric, and then remove the pattern.

2. Cut out the armature pattern, and pin or baste it to the single-layer piece of armature fabric. Cut out the fabric, and then remove the pattern. Place the armature pattern on the lightweight cardboard, and trace. Cut out the cardboard just inside the traced line.

3. Cover one side of the cardboard armature with a very thin layer of fabric glue, and place the cardboard in the middle of the fabric armature piece. Firmly press the pieces together. Let dry.

4. Take the joined fabric and cardboard armature piece, and glue the fabric side to the inside of the rear body piece. Let dry.

ASSEMBLING THE DOLL

5. Lay the front body piece on top of the rear body piece, and pin or baste it into place. Starting at the top of the doll's neck, stitch around the doll until you reach the top of its second "arm."

6. Gently place a little stuffing between the front body piece and the cardboard armature piece. The doll should be about $3/4$ inch (1.9 cm) thick at the center. Sew the doll closed.

CREATING THE HEAD, HANDS, & FEET

7. Place the head pattern on doubled fabric, right sides together, trace, remove the pattern, and cut out.

8. Pin the two head pieces to the body, one on the front and one on the back of the neck point. Starting at the top of the head, use a stab stitch to join the head pieces together. When you reach the cardboard armature and cannot sew straight though all layers, use a running stitch to sew past the cardboard, and then return to the stab stitch to sew the remainder. Firmly stuff the head before sewing the last $1/2$ inch (1.3 cm) of fabric together.

9. Repeat steps 7 and 8 to create, attach, and stuff the hands and feet.

DOLLS
for
Personal Growth

Some dollmakers recognize that while working mindfully with their hands, they can reach deep into their souls and engage themselves at a mystical level. These doll artists cherish their creations as friends who guide and encourage them, filling them with delight and inspiration.

People of different backgrounds, many with little artistic experience, are currently making dolls as therapy. Often meeting in groups, they build their dolls as they talk and share personal stories. The participants let their dolls lead them on a journey of healing and self-discovery. Infused with the energy of their creators, these dolls have the power to transform lives. Making them helps people come to terms with (and mend) pain and loss, or deal with deep-rooted fears.

Tracy Stilwell's
CLARITY

Mixing media adds up to more than the sum of its parts. Here, the artist has pieced fabric in the manner of crazy quilting to form the foundation fabric. Embroidery stitches in a variety of threads add more color, texture, pattern, and depth. Polymer clay, twisted wire, and beads top it off in high style.

CREATING THE BODY FABRIC

1. Arrange small scraps of coordinating fabrics on top of the background fabric, making a pleasing design. Machine-stitch the fabric scraps onto the foundation. Further embellish the surface if desired with decorative machine stitching.

what you need

Basic sewing kit

1/2 yard (45.7 cm) of fabric for background, light- or medium-weight cotton

Small coordinating fabric scraps

Photocopied doll patterns (body only), pages 134–135

Lightweight cardboard for armature

Embroidery thread

Charms for hands

Metallic thread

Polymer clay

Colored plastic-coated wire

Decorative beads

ASSEMBLING THE DOLL

2. Cut out the photocopied body pattern. Place it on top of the patched fabric, and pin the pattern in place. Draw around the pattern with a soft lead pencil or a disappearing fabric marker. Remove the pattern.

3. Place the body pattern on a single layer of the background fabric. Pin the pattern in place. Trace, and then remove the pattern. Baste together the two pieces of body fabric, right sides together.

4. Follow steps 3 and 4 of the basic pattern for Clarity (woven fabrics) on page 33. Clip the corners and the curves, and then turn the fabric right side out.

5. Cut out the photocopied body armature pattern, and transfer it onto cardboard. Insert the cardboard armature into the body, pressing it to the rear.

6. Follow step 6 of the basic pattern for Clarity (woven fabrics) .

EMBELLISHING THE BODY

7. Select certain areas on the front of the body to embroider. Use assorted stitches and thread colors in a fashion similar to the "crazy quilt" finishing technique.

8. Use metallic thread to stitch the hand charms to the ends of the arms. Make several loops around the charms to secure. After knotting, leave extra-long thread tails for decoration.

CREATING & ATTACHING THE FACE

9. Sculpt a three-dimensional face from polymer clay, leaving the back of the head flat. Create a hole through the clay on each side of the face, near the cheek. Twist the colored wires to make the hair. Insert the wires into the clay prior to baking. Follow the manufacturer's instructions for working with and baking the clay.

10. Color the face as desired after baking the clay. Use the metallic thread to sew the face onto the neck through the cheek holes. Attach a bead at each hole if desired. After knotting, leave extra-long thread tails for decoration.

Lynne Sward's
CLARITY

Make your own dream doll, and fill it with your secret wishes. The hidden pocket on this doll is handy for doing just that. You also could keep a small pencil in the pocket to record your dreams, or personalize the flap for an extraordinary tooth-fairy pillow.

CREATING THE POCKET & FLAP

1. Cut out the photocopied flap pattern. Transfer the pattern onto lightweight cardboard, and cut it out.

what you need

Basic sewing kit

Photocopied flap and pocket pattern, page 136

Photocopied doll patterns, page 134

Lightweight cardboard

½ yard (45.7 cm) commercial dyed cotton fabric for body and flap

6 x 6 inches (15.2 x 15.2 cm) muslin

6 x 6 inches (15.2 x 15.2 cm) transparent fabric

Variegated rayon machine thread

Metallic sewing machine thread

Glass seed beads

Sequins

Embroidery thread

Hand-dyed rayon yarn

Gold-plated star charm

2. Create a three-layer fabric sandwich with the cotton foundation fabric on the bottom, the muslin in the middle, and the transparent fabric on the top. (You can add more transparent fabric scraps to the top if you like.)

3. Machine-embroider all layers of fabric together. Trace the flap pattern template onto the sewn fabric, then trim the fabric to the shape of the doll design. Finish the edges of the flap fabric using a variegated rayon thread and a satin stitch on your machine.

ASSEMBLING THE DOLL

4. Follow steps 1, 2, and 3 of the basic pattern for Clarity (woven fabrics) on page 33.

5. Cut out the photocopied body armature pattern, and transfer it onto light cardboard. Cut out the armature and insert it into the back of the body.

6. Lightly stuff the fabric between the cardboard and the front body piece. Turn in the open edges on the top of the doll, and pin in place. Hand-stitch the doll to close.

7. Sew the flap to the front of the doll by hand using an overcast stitch.

CREATING THE FACE & HAIR

8. Cut out the photocopied face pattern. Trace it onto the face fabric. Draw the facial features onto the fabric with dressmaker's chalk. Hand-sew the beads onto the fabric three at a time, and then anchor them with a backstitch.

9. Sew around the face, right sides together, leaving an opening. Cut out the face ¼ inch (6 mm) from the seam and opening. Turn the fabric right side out. Stuff the face. Turn in the open edges, then hand-stitch to close. Hand-sew the face to the neck.

10. Hand-tack loops of the hand-dyed rayon yarn to make the hair. Sew the star charm onto the top of the head.

FINISHING THE DOLL

11. Draw the text on the front of the flap with dressmaker's chalk. Embroider the words onto the flap using a backstitch and embroidery and sewing machine threads.

12. Create the secret pocket in the same manner as the front flap (refer to steps 1, 2, and 3). Attach the pocket to the doll under the flap, using overhand stitches. Sew a small hanging strip onto the back of the doll so it can be wall-mounted.

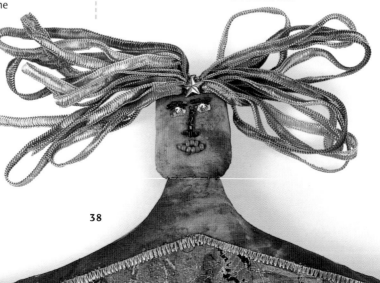

Arlinka Blair's
CLARITY

Arlinka Blair's fabric choices are inspired by ancient cultures. Her intriguing serpent design resembles the primitive cave paintings discovered by archaeologists. Clarity's width is a wonderful surface for this fusion of linoleum–block printing and handsome embroidery accents.

CARVING THE LINOLEUM BLOCK

1. Make a carbon-copy transfer of the photocopied serpent pattern (or your own sketch) onto the linoleum block.

what you need

Basic sewing kit

Photocopied serpent template, page 137

Carbon paper

Linoleum block

Linoleum cutters

Fabric printing ink, black

Ink roller

Smooth surface for spreading ink, such as clear plastic sheeting

Two 9½ x 10-inch (24.1 x 25.4 cm) pieces of fabric for body

Photocopied doll patterns, pages 134–135

9½ x 10-inch (24.1 x 25.4 cm) piece of light cardboard for armature

Small scraps of coordinating patterned fabric for head, feet, and hands

Embroidery thread, three or more colors

2. Use the linoleum cutters to carve out the areas on the block that won't hold ink.

BLOCK PRINTING THE BODY FABRIC

3. Prepare the fabric ink for block printing according to the manufacturer's directions. Use the ink roller to spread a small amount of ink on the clear plastic sheeting or other smooth surface.

4. After the roller is coated with ink, spread an even amount onto the carved linoleum block. To test the print, carefully place the block face down on a piece of paper. Press down firmly without sliding the block. Carefully lift the block off the paper. If necessary, continue to carve and test-print until you're satisfied with the results.

5. Make a linoleum-block print onto the front piece of the body fabric. Let the ink dry.

PREPARING THE PATTERN PIECES

6. Cut out the photocopied body pattern, and place it on top of the printed fabric. Pin the pattern in place. Trace the pattern with a soft lead pencil or a disappearing fabric marker. Remove the pattern.

7. Place the body pattern on top of the rear body fabric. Pin the pattern in place, then trace it with a soft lead pencil or a disappearing fabric marker.

8. Cut out both body pieces. Baste them together, right sides together. Cut out the photocopied armature pattern, and trace it onto the cardboard. Cut out the cardboard inside the marked line.

CONSTRUCTING THE DOLL

9. Follow steps 3 through 10 of the basic pattern for Clarity (woven fabrics) on page 33.

EMBELLISHING THE FABRIC

10. Embroider around the serpent block print in a dark color thread. Use a bold stitch that enhances the outline. Embroider inside the eyes and add facial features as desired.

11. Use embroidery threads in coordinating colors to make a single row of fringe across the top seam of the head. To make the fringe, insert a needle just below the seam on one side of the head and gently pull it through. Leave at least 2 inches (5 cm) of thread trailing the insertion. Loop the needle back over the seam and re-insert it near the original piercing. Tightly pull the thread through to the other side. Clip the thread for the length of fringe desired. Continue to fringe across the seam line from neck edge to neck edge, alternating the thread colors.

12. Make a ½- to 1-inch (1.3 to 2.5 cm) row of embroidery-thread fringe at the lower seam of the body. Start the fringe approximately two-thirds of the distance from the hands to the feet. Refer to step 11 for instructions on making fringe.

13. Using a thin, dark-colored floss, sew a decorative border around the contour of the face. Accentuate individual pattern sections with decorative stitching to form blocks of color. These blocks should resemble facial features.

14. Repeat step 13 on the hands and feet, making more delicate decorative stitches.

Pamela Hastings'
CLARITY

Ethereal colors and patterns, including some heavenly batiks, give this doll its angelic glow. To make her really fly, the artist added wings to the basic pattern and an amazing head of hair. Take your time choosing just the right fabrics for your cherub.

PIECING THE BODY FABRIC

1. Measure, mark, and cut a 3 x 11-inch (7.6 x 27.9 cm) strip from the most interesting fabric. This is the front vertical panel for the body. For the side panels, cut two 3¹/₂ x 4¹/₂-inch (8.9 x 11.4 cm) strips, two 2 x 4-inch (5 x 10.2 cm) strips, and two 2¹/₂ x 5¹/₂-inch (6.4 x 14 cm) strips.

what you need

Basic sewing kit

*6 fat quarters of coordinating cottons

Photocopied doll pattern, page 138

Lightweight cardboard for armature

Photocopied wing patterns, page 139

Photocopied face and hand patterns, page 139

Embroidery threads, several coordinating shades

Strands of fuzzy yarn for hair, several colors and textures, each about 12 inches (30.5 cm) long

Tiny pearls or beads

Clear monofilament or decorative ribbon for hanging

*A fat quarter is a fabric term familiar to quilters. It refers to the method of cutting a quarter of 1 yard (91.4 cm) of fabric from a bolt of cloth. If you were to roll out and cut 9 inches (22.9 cm) of fabric you would end up with a long and narrow strip. However, if you roll out one entire yard (91.4 cm), and cut that amount into quarters, the result is a much more useful, nearly square piece of fabric.

2. Using a ¹/₄-inch (6 mm) seam allowance, sew the side panels together, as shown in figure 1. The left panel has its straight vertical edge on the right side; the right panel has its straight vertical edge on the left side. Iron the pieced fabric.

3. Sew the pieced side panels to the correct side of the center strip, matching their edges at the bottom, right sides together. Iron the pieced fabric.

ASSEMBLING THE BODY

4. Cut out the photocopied body pattern. Trace the body pattern on the wrong side of the pieced front panel.

5. On another fabric, measure and cut out an 11 x 11-inch (27.9 x 27.9 cm) square. Pin the pieced front panel to the new fabric square, right sides together. Sew from hand to hand around the bottom edge with a ¹/₄-inch (6 mm) seam. Sew a second seam just outside the first one. Trim the fabric and clip the curves. Press and turn the doll.

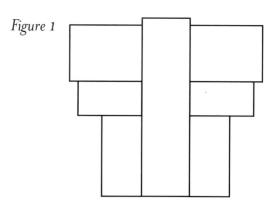

Figure 1

6. Cut out the photocopied patterns for the body and wing armatures. Trace the patterns onto poster board or thin cardboard, and cut out. Insert the body cardboard armature into the turned body, making sure it goes down into the feet. Lightly stuff the doll between the cardboard and the front piece.

7. Pin each side of the open fabric over the shoulders. On the front edge of the open fabric, turn under a ¹/₄-inch (6 mm) hem that overlaps the back body fabric. Slip-stitch the top edge closed. (If you choose to embroider the edge, it's easier to manage if the edge is slip-stitched first.)

Figure 2

PIECING THE WING FABRIC

8. Measure, mark, and cut one 5 1/2 x 3 3/4-inch (14 cm x 9.5 cm) fabric strip for the top of each wing. Measure, mark, and cut three 2 x 5-inch (5 x 12.7 cm) fabric strips for each of the bottom wing panels. You have four strips for each wing, each cut from a different fabric.

9. Using a 1/4-inch (6 mm) seam allowance, sew the bottom wing panels together, as shown in figure 2. Iron the pieced fabric.

10. Sew the bottom wing panels to the top portion of the wing, right sides together. Remember to reverse the color progression when you attach the bottom wing panel to the top. Iron the fabric.

ASSEMBLING THE WINGS

11. Cut out the photocopied wing pattern, and trace it on the wrong side of the pieced wing panels. Lay the wing panel on the same fabric used for the back of the body, right sides together.

12. Sew the pieced wing panel to the wing back, leaving open the space from point A to point B. Press the wings, trim the seams, and turn.

13. Insert one cardboard armature into each wing, bending the cardboard slightly so it fits through the opening. Lightly stuff in front of the cardboard. Pin the open wing edges, and then slip stitch to close.

FORMING THE FACE & HANDS

14. For the face and hands, measure, mark, and cut a 3 1/2 x 10-inch (8.9 x 25.4 cm) fabric strip. Fold the strip in half, right sides together, and iron. Draw one face and two hands on the wrong side of the fabric. Stitch each piece, leaving an opening for turning and stuffing. Iron the fabric, trim the seams, and turn. Stuff the head and hands, and then slip stitch closed.

15. Use a running stitch to embroider a simple face. For hair, attach several strands of fuzzy yarn in the center of the head with embroidery floss. Use a ladder stitch to sew the head to the top of the body. Trim the hair attractively.

16. Sew the hands to the ends of the arms. Embellish the body and wings as desired with embroidery floss and small beads.

ATTACHING THE WINGS & HANGING MATERIAL

17. Pin the wings to the back of the body with the longer, pointed ends on top. Use a ladder stitch to attach the wings, almost perpendicular to the back of the body.

18. Attach a strand of monofilament or a decorative ribbon to each of the wings, and tie above the doll, so it can hang from a hook. To determine where to attach the hanging lines to the wings, tie two pieces of string around two pins. Place the pins in different locations on the wings. The doll will hang more or less forward, depending on its center of gravity.

Barbara Carleton Evans'
CLARITY

Here's a creative way to live out your cowgirl fantasies. This desert dreamscape is made of felt appliques in sunset shades. The artist took advantage of Clarity's wide-open surface to express a thematic concept. Follow her lead, or blaze your own artistic trail.

PREPARING THE PATTERN PIECES

1. Cut out the photocopied body and head pattern pieces, and baste them to doubled felt. Cut out the felt; then remove the pattern.

2. Cut out the armature pattern piece, and pin or baste it to a single layer of armature felt. Cut out the felt, and then remove the pattern. Trace the armature pattern onto cardboard. Cut out the cardboard just inside the traced line.

what you need

Basic sewing kit

Photocopied doll patterns, pages 134–135

Two 9½ x 10-inch (24.1 x 25.4 cm) pieces of felt for body

9½ x 10-inch (24.1 x 25.4 cm) piece of felt for armature

9½ x 10-inch (24.1 x 25.4 cm) piece of lightweight cardboard for armature

Fabric glue

Assorted felt scraps for applique

Photocopied applique patterns, page 140

Embroidery threads

Metal charms

3. Cover one side of the cardboard armature with a thin layer of fabric glue, and place it in the middle of the felt armature piece. Firmly press the pieces together. Let dry.

CREATING & ATTACHING THE APPLIQUES

4. Cut out the photocopied applique patterns, and pin them onto felt. Trace the applique shapes onto the felt, and cut out.

5. Position the gloves on the doll. Spread a thin layer of flexible fabric glue on the back of the part to be fringed. Let the glue dry before cutting the fringe.

6. Make the sun separately, and add it to the doll after it's sewed. Stack the three sun pieces. Baste or hold them together with a tiny dot of glue. Using embroidery stitches, make lines on top of the stack to represent sun rays.

7. Position the remaining appliques on top of the front body piece. Affix them with tiny drops of fabric glue. Use embroidery threads to embellish and define the appliques with decorative stitching.

8. Attach each horse's mane and tail at its base. Separate the strands of thread, and glue them in place.

9. Sew on the body charms, leaving a tail on the thread.

ASSEMBLING THE DOLL

10. Glue the felt side of the armature piece to the inside of the rear body piece. Let dry.

11. Pin or baste the front body piece to the rear body piece. Starting at the top of the neck, stitch around the doll's edge until you reach the top of the second glove.

12. Follow steps 6, 7, and 8 of the basic pattern for Clarity (nonwoven fabrics) on page 34.

ADDING THE FINAL TOUCHES

13. Attach charms to opposite sides of the head for hair.

14. Embroider a hat band onto the front hat piece. Leaving the bottom of the hat open, embroider around the upper part of the brim and the crown. Put the hat on the doll's head, and glue in place.

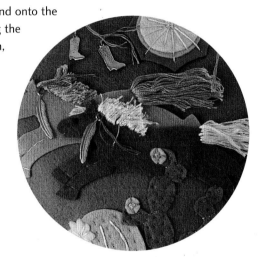

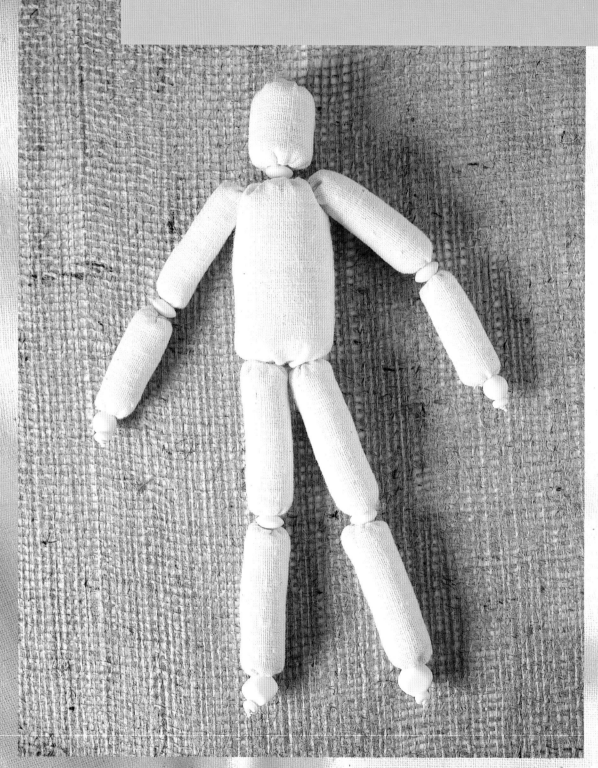

MAKING THE BODY PARTS

1. Cut out the photocopied pattern pieces, pin them to the wrong side of the body fabrics, and trace. Remove the pattern from the fabric, and cut out the cloth on the traced lines.

what you need

Basic sewing kit

Photocopied doll patterns, page 144

1/2 yard (45.7 cm) or large scraps of fabric(s) for body parts

Heavy linen or upholstery thread for stringing

9 or more beads or buttons for neck, hands, feet, and elbow and knee joints

Fabric glue, optional

TIP

The best fabric for making this doll is a firmly woven cloth with very little stretch in any direction. If you're working with a fabric that might ravel when you turn and gather, machine-stitch across the open ends before stitching the side seams.

2. Fold the fabric for the head in half with the right sides together. Sew the short edges together to form a tube. Fold the fabric for the body in half with the right sides together. Sew the short edges together to make a tube. Fold the fabric rectangles for the arm and leg pieces in half with the right sides together. Sew the long edges together to make individual tubes. Turn all the tubes right side out.

3. For each body part, tightly gather one end, tucking the raw edges inside the tube. Hand-sew the gathered end to close. (When using a very stiff fabric, it helps to turn in a hem and pin it into place before gathering.)

4. Firmly stuff all body parts. Gather the open end of each stuffed body part, tuck all raw fabric edges to the inside, and hand-sew closed.

ASSEMBLING THE HEAD, BODY & LEGS

5. Using a dollmaker's needle and heavy linen or upholstery thread, assemble the doll by stringing the body parts together following the sequence illustrated in figure 1. Cut two pieces of thread that are twice the length of the doll plus 6 inches (15.2 cm). Sew the doll together in the following order: after inserting the needle into the top of the doll's head, push it out the neck, through the neck button(s) or bead(s), down through the body, into the upper leg, through the knee button(s) or bead(s), into the lower leg, out at the ankle, and through the foot button(s) or bead(s).

6. Turn the needle around and work it back through the foot button(s) or bead(s), then through the body and buttons or beads in reverse order. Bring the needle out of the top of the head 1/8 inch (3 mm) from where it initially went in. Leave the stringing thread for the first side very loose until you string the second side.

7. Repeat steps 5 and 6 to string the other side of the doll. Once complete, pull the threads so the body parts on both sides are snug against each other. Tie the threads together in a square knot, adding a touch of glue if desired.

ATTACHING THE ARMS

8. Cut two pieces of thread that are four times the length of the arm plus 8 inches (20.3 cm). Put the point of the needle into the body just under the neck button or bead, and bring it out at the same point on the opposite side. Insert the needle into the top of the upper arm, come out at the elbow, pass through the elbow button(s) or bead(s), down through the lower arm, through the hand button(s) or bead(s), and then back up through the arm in reverse order.

9. Put the point of the needle into the body just under the neck button or bead, and bring it out at the same point on the opposite side where you started. Pull the thread until the arm is tight against the body, and tie it off with a square knot.

10. Repeat steps 8 and 9 on the opposite side of the body to string the second arm. Trim the ends of the thread, or leave them long and use the thread to tie on embellishments. (You can disguise the knots and trimmed thread by adding a touch of glue and pressing them down on the fabric.)

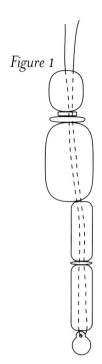

Figure 1

ALTERNATE PATTERN SUGGESTIONS

• It's easy to enlarge, reduce, or otherwise modify the size of this pattern to accommodate different body fabrics and your design concept (see Tracy Stilwell's interpretation on page 57). If you choose to use stiff or heavy fabrics, definitely make the body parts larger.

• Non-woven fabrics may be used, but the body parts will have to be quite large to gather properly at the ends. Even then, the gathers may have to be covered with larger disk beads or buttons.

• Here's a different method for making body parts out of one piece of fabric (they'll all be the same diameter):

1. Cut a long strip of fabric, and fold it in half lengthwise with the right sides together.

2. Stitch down the length of the strip. Trim the fabric, leaving a seam allowance.

3. Mark a line indicating the length of each body part. Squeeze a line of seam sealant onto the fabric where marked, and let dry.

4. Cut out the body parts at the marked lines. Turn the tubes right side out.

5. Gather and stitch one end of each body part. Firmly stuff, gather, and stitch the second end closed.

DOLLS
for
Good Health

For centuries, cultures from around the world have used dolls as health insurance, and as surrogates for both healthy and sick people.

The Navaho American Indians believed that an unborn child might be injured if its mother saw a wounded animal or blood during her pregnancy. To prevent this injury, a Navaho medicine man carved a human figure out of wood during a brief ceremony, and placed it somewhere accessible to the supernatural spirits they believed were sent to harm the baby. Duped, the spirits would act upon the doll instead of the baby.

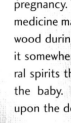

Japanese children who played with special dolls made of clay were supposed to grow up healthy (and wealthy, as well.) A sick child might receive a doll as a scapegoat, to cause the disease to leave the child and enter the doll. In parts of Japan and China, paper dolls representing each family member were ceremoniously inflicted with every possible disease, then tossed into a fire to ensure that the illnesses would never afflict the people.

Many collections of antique medical paraphenalia number Chinese doctor dolls among their artifacts. Modesty prevented a woman from mentioning parts of her body to her physician, so doctor dolls were used to indicate where on the body the woman felt pain. Male Chinese physicians were forbidden to touch female patients. Ladies of rank weren't even seen by their doctors. The doctor's diagnosis was made on the basis of the doll. Ranging from 5 to 13 inches (12.7 to 33 cm) in length, these dolls depicted a nude or draped woman reclining on one side, with one arm behind her head and the hair brushed back from the forehead. Because Chinese women kept their feet covered at all times, even in the presence of their husbands, the dolls usually wore slippers. Most often carved of ivory, these valued dolls also were made of jade, lapis lazuli, alabaster, and rosewood.

Barbara Carleton Evans'
ENERGY

Intense colors really make this doll come to life. Stringing more beads at the shoulders increases arm mobility. Coordinating striped body fabrics run horizontally on the torso and arms and vertically on the legs. Vibrant joint buttons and hair yarn tie the whole look together.

MAKING THE BODY PARTS

1. Follow steps 1 through 4 of the basic pattern for Energy on page 47.

STRINGING THE DOLL

2. String the head, torso, and legs together using a dollmaker's needle and linen or upholstery thread. Use two buttons for the neck and each knee joint and a large shank button for each foot. Refer to steps 5, 6, and 7 of the basic pattern for stringing order.

what you need

Basic sewing kit

Photocopied doll patterns, page 144

1/2 yard (45.7 cm) of fabric for body

Linen or upholstery thread for stringing

6 large buttons for neck and knees

2 large shank buttons for feet

6 small buttons for elbows and shoulders

10–12 small beads for shoulders

2 small shank buttons for hands

2 extra-large buttons for face

Wire coathanger

Wire cutters

Yarn for hair

Fabric glue, optional

3. Cut two pieces of stringing thread that are four times the length of the arm plus 8 inches (20.3 cm). As shown in figure 1, insert the needle into the top of the upper arm, come out at the elbow, pass through the elbow buttons, down through the lower arm, through the small shank hand button, and then back up through the arm in reverse order.

4. Sew a small button to the shoulder. Pull the ends of the stringing thread to hold the arm parts together. String enough small beads on each end to go from the shoulder to the neck

Figure 1

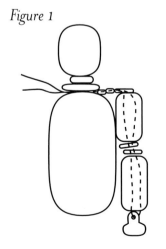

buttons. (You may have to unthread the needle to do this.)

5. Put the point of the needle into the body just under the neck button, and bring it out at the same point on the opposite side. Pull the thread until the arm is tight against the body, and tie off.

6. Repeat steps 3, 4, and 5 to string the second arm. Trim the ends of the thread. You can further disguise the knots and trimmed thread by adding a touch of glue and pressing them down on the fabric.

ADDING THE FACE BUTTONS

7. Anchor the thread at the back of the head. Sew through the head and through the extra large buttons; then put the needle through the back of the head. Knot the thread.

MAKING THE HAIR

8. Figure 2 shows you how to make an easy hair loom. Cut a wire coat hanger just next to the center. Use the smaller U-shape part of the hanger. Bend the wires so they are the same distance apart. Wrap the wires with yarn starting at the open end of the U and working toward the closed end.

Figure 2

9. Place the open end of the U-shape wire under the sewing machine's presser foot, and sew up the center of the wrapped yarn. Pause after sewing 2 to 3 inches (5 to 7.6 cm), put the presser foot down, and pull the loom towards you. Keep wrapping the yarn and sewing until you have enough hair to cover the head. Hand-stitch the hair to the top of the head.

Arlinka Blair's
ENERGY

Leader, healer, dancer, or sage—this shamanistic figure radiates spiritual energy. The earthy body fabrics are a splendid array of deep, rich colors and textures. Airy veils add an ethereal dimension. Choose a single color theme, and make one doll for each of the earth's elements: fire, earth, air, and water.

PREPARING THE PATTERN PIECES

1. Cut out the photocopied pattern pieces. Determine which fabric you'd like to use for each body part. Pin or baste the pattern pieces to the wrong side of the fabrics. Cut out the cloth for all the pattern pieces.

MAKING & ASSEMBLING THE BODY PARTS

2. Follow steps 2 through 4 of the basic pattern for Energy on page 47.

3. String the body parts together using a dollmaker's needle and linen or upholstery thread. Use two metal beads per beaded joint. Refer to steps 5 through 10 of the basic pattern for Energy for stringing order.

CREATING & ATTACHING FABRIC AND YARN STRIPS

4. Tear or collect thin strips of fabric or ragged-edged ribbons, each approximately 3 to 4 inches (7.6 to 10.2 cm) long. Select many different but coordinating colors and textures.

5. Choose two or three fabric or ribbon strips, and tie them between the neck beads. The strip ends should fall at various lengths. Assemble four more groups of fabric or ribbon strips. Tie one group to each shoulder joint and one to each upper leg joint.

6. Make two bundles of interesting yarn fibers. Tie one bundle around each lower leg joint between the two metal beads.

ADDING THE MILAGROS OR CHARMS

7. Sew an individual milagro or charm to the end of each arm and leg with embroidery thread to create the hands and feet. Use many stitches to secure each milagro to the doll. Let the stitches remain visible, and when you're finished, trim the thread about 1 inch (2.5 cm) away from the knot.

8. To make the mask, sew a milagro or charm to the front of the head with embroidery thread. Fasten the mask to the doll with many stitches.

CREATING THE HAIR

9. Make a single row of fringe at the top of the mask with embroidery threads. To make the fringe, insert the needle and gently pull it through. Leave at least 2 inches (5 cm) of thread trailing the insertion. Loop the needle back over the seam and re-insert it near the original piercing. Tightly pull the thread through to the other side. Repeat this process to make more fringe. Clip the thread to the desired length.

ADDING DECORATIVE STITCHING

10. Use a dark thread and a straight but irregular embroidery stitch to add texture to the front surface of the body. Decorate the face below the mask and the surface of one upper leg with embroidery thread. Sew a loop made of heavy thread onto the back of the head for hanging.

what you need

Basic sewing kit

Photocopied doll patterns, page 144

Assorted small fabric scraps for body parts

10 metal beads

Assorted fabric strips and ribbons

Unusual yarn fibers

*Milagros or charms

Embroidery threads

*Milagros (Spanish for "miracles") are found throughout Latin America, offered by the hundreds of thousands of devoted petitioners whose purchase or fabrication of these votive offerings continues an ancient folk practice. The small metal charms represent different parts of the body or of the spirit. They are used as petitions for miracles to be performed, or in gratitude for miracles already enacted. The petitioner buys the milagros at or near a church or shrine. A ribbon or pin is slipped through the loop of the milagro, and it's pinned to the skirts of the church's patron saint or placed on a statue. Milagros, both contemporary and antique, can be found at bead and jewelry suppliers.

Pamela Hastings'
ENERGY

Have you ever wanted your own robot, or to meet an outer space android? The future is now.
This doll springs to life thanks to a graphic pattern of radiant ribbons, contrasting topstitching, and
bright buttons and beads. You don't need a laboratory to make this timely doll; just loosen up your
sci-fi imagination.

ARRANGING THE FABRIC & RIBBON

1. Cut out the photocopied patterns. Trace them onto the wrong side of the body fabric, and then cut out on the marked lines. Lay the body parts flat on your work surface in the proper formation and right side up.

what you need

Basic sewing kit

Photocopied doll patterns, page 144

1 fat quarter tightly woven cotton, subtle dark pattern

Fabric glue

$1/4$-inch-wide (6 mm) satin ribbon in 4 bright colors, about 1 yard (91.4 cm) each

8 buttons, $3/4$ inch (1.9 cm) in diameter

12 buttons, $1/2$ inch (1.3 cm) in diameter

5 beads, $1/4$ inch (6 mm) in diameter

5 pony beads for eyes and mouth

2. Use the fabric glue to spot-attach lengths of the satin ribbon to the fabric rectangles in a geometric pattern (see figure 1). Let the glue dry. In this project, the yellow ribbon runs lengthwise down the center of each body piece, acting as a unifying element. The limb ribbons match side to side, and the rust-colored ribbon acts as eyebrows. Purple ribbon highlights the doll's eyes, shoulders, and hips.

STITCHING THE RIBBON

3. Using a thread that coordinates with the body fabric, topstitch down each ribbon as shown in figure 1, stitching close to both edges.

4. Topstitch back and forth across each piece of the dark fabric as illustrated in figure 1, using a bright thread that matches one of the ribbons. This adds unity and another texture. During this process, you don't need to change the bobbin thread. Carefully press the fabric.

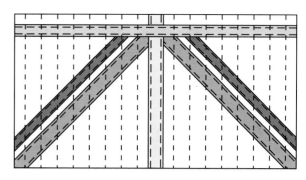

Figure 1

MAKING THE BODY PARTS

5. Follow steps 2 through 4 of the basic pattern for Energy on page 47.

ASSEMBLING THE DOLL

6. String the body parts together with a heavy bright-colored thread. Using a regular sewing needle, start at the five outside points (the ends of the four limbs and the top of the head), and work your way into the body. Tie off the thread where it's hidden under a button. Use two $3/4$-inch (1.9 cm) buttons for the neck and each hip joint and one $3/4$-inch (1.9 cm) button for each shoulder joint and the top of the head. Use single $1/2$-inch (1.3 cm) buttons for the hands, elbows, and knees. Use double $1/2$-inch (1.3 cm) buttons for the feet.

7. Sew a $1/4$-inch (6 mm) bead to the ends of the hands and feet and on top of the head.

8. Sew pony beads to the face to create the eyes and mouth.

Lynne Sward's
ENERGY

*Bold black-and-white graphics on top of a rainbow of color make this doll unusually animated.
Bead-fringed fingers and toes give her a festive air. The fabric pattern is an original design drawn by
the artist and transferred to the cloth. Here's the perfect opportunity to turn your doodles into art.*

DESIGNING THE FABRIC

1. Create an original design for the body fabric by making a drawing on white paper. Make doodles, patterns, write words, or draw any other graphic pattern. Draw your own image for the face. Take these drawings to a print shop, and have them photocopied onto specially-coated transfer paper. Have the photocopy transferred onto the cotton fabric at the print shop, or do it at home with a hot iron.

what you need

Basic sewing kit

Drawing paper, white

Drawing pens or pencils

1/2 yard (45.7 cm) of cotton fabric

Photocopied doll patterns, page 144

Polymer clay, 2 or 3 colors

Heavy linen or upholstery thread

Beading needle and thread

Glass seed beads

Dyed pearl cotton thread

2 x 5 inches (5 x 12.7 cm) of coordinating fabric for skirt

2 x 5 inches (5 x 12.7 cm) of coordinating chiffon for skirt

MAKING THE BODY PARTS

2. Follow steps 1 through 4 of the basic pattern for Energy on page 47.

CREATING THE BEADS

3. Use the polymer clay to make five beads to string between the limbs. Knead together two or more colors of polymer clay to produce the simple marbling effect shown here. Sculpt the beads to your liking, and allow them to dry according to the clay manufacturer's recommendations.

ASSEMBLING THE DOLL

4. Follow steps 5 through 10 of the basic pattern for Energy on page 47. (Single beads won't be used for hands or feet).

EMBELLISHING THE FACE

5. Using a beading needle and thread, sew the glass seed beads around the head to frame the face, backstitching onto the fabric.

6. Use pinking shears to cut pointed strips of hair like those shown in figure 1. Sew the strips together, wrong sides facing, using a zigzag stitch. Stuff the hair into the head opening, and hand-sew closed.

7. Hand-sew the embroidery pearl cotton and machine thread for hair around the face.

MAKING THE SKIRT

8. Hand-draw symbols onto a 2 x 5-inch (5 x 12.7 cm) piece of coordinating fabric. Layer the marked fabric on top of the chiffon and accent fabric pieces. Turn under one edge of the layered fabric, and secure it in place with a zigzag stitch.

9. Cut the skirt's lower edge to look like fringe. Topstitch the skirt onto the body.

MAKING THE HANDS & FEET

10. You'll use a bead-fringe technique to make the hands and feet. As shown in figure 2, first anchor the beading needle into the fabric. String any number of glass seed beads. Turn the needle around, then sew back up the string of beads and into the fabric. Repeat this step to make 10 fingers and toes.

Figure 1

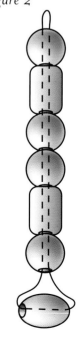

Figure 2

Tracy Stilwell's
ENERGY

Here's a great example of altering a doll pattern to make it your own. The artist lengthened the legs, shortened the arms, and enlarged the diameter of the body parts to match her vision. The body fabric is hand-dyed, making it one-of-a-kind. The face is polymer clay fashioned to look like carved ivory.

COLORING THE FABRIC

1. Use diluted fabric paints to make a wash of colors over the cotton fabric. To create soft shifts in color, let the thin paints run and bleed into each other. Let the fabric dry.

what you need

Basic sewing kit

Fabric paints

Paintbrush

1/2 yard (45.7 cm) of light-colored cotton fabric for body

Linen or upholstery thread

18 buttons for neck, hands, and elbow and hip joints, 1/2 to 1 inch (1.3 to 2.5 cm) in diameter

Patterned cotton fabric scraps for applique and wraps

Embroidery thread

Polymer clay, white or off-white

Carving tool

Acrylic paint, black and brown

Sandpaper

Coarse flax-colored yarn

Multi-colored yarn

MAKING THE BODY PARTS

2. Instead of making several individual tubes, the artist created one large tube for each arm and leg, and then gathered the fabric at different lengths. To create your doll this way, measure, mark, and cut the dyed cotton fabric to the following measurements: one 2 x 3-inch (5 x 7.6 cm) rectangle for the head; one 3 1/2 x 4-inch (8.9 x 10.2 cm) rectangle for the body; two 3 x 7-inch (7.6 x 17.8 cm) rectangles for the legs; and two 3 x 3-inch (7.6 x 7.6 cm) squares for the arms.

3. Follow steps 2, 3, and 4 of the basic pattern for Energy on page 47.

ASSEMBLING THE DOLL

4. String the body parts together using a dollmaker's needle and heavy linen or upholstery thread. If needed, refer to the stringing order and guide on page 47, steps 5 through 10. This doll uses four buttons to make a long neck between the head and body, two buttons at each shoulder, and one button on the end of each arm. Four buttons are strung between the body and each leg to form hip joints.

MAKING ELBOW & KNEE JOINTS

5. Anchor the strong thread at the center point of one arm. Tightly wrap the thread around the limb several times to divide the tube into two parts. Repeat this process on the second arm.

6. Anchor the strong thread at the center point of one leg. Tightly wrap the thread around the limb several times to divide the tube into two parts. Anchor the thread between the top of the leg and the center gather. Tightly wrap the thread around the limb several times to divide the tube into three parts. Anchor the thread between the bottom of the leg and the center gather. Tightly wrap the thread around the limb several times to divide the tube into four parts. Repeat this process on the second leg.

ADDING FABRIC ACCENTS

7. Make eight narrow strips from the patterned cotton fabric. Sew one strip around each gather on all limbs.

8. Cut out a symbol, in this case a heart, from the patterned cotton fabric to adorn the doll body. Applique the fabric to the front of the body with embroidery thread.

CREATING THE FACE & HAIR

9. Use polymer clay to create a flat form for the doll's face. To make the facial features, carve lines into the soft clay. Follow the manufacturer's instructions for working with and baking the clay.

10. To replicate the look of ivory, paint the carved lines black, rub the whole polymer clay surface with brown paint, and then sand the face with fine sandpaper. Repeat rubbing paint on and sanding the face until you achieve the look you desire. Adhere the face to the front surface of the head with fabric glue.

11. Gather strands of coarse flax-colored yarn, and stitch them directly onto the top of the head. Add a few strands of multi-colored yarns to the hair.

DOLLS
for
Sacrifice

Dolls have to be fairly robust to stand up to the rigors of a child's play. Sometimes, dolls also have to take the punishment that humans seek to escape.

In England and Germany, parents once placed changeling dolls in baby cradles. These dolls were meant to deceive witches and fairies who, the parents thought, would attempt to snatch their much-prized human babies, leaving behind their own grotesque offspring.

During the Sassiva Festival in India, girls throw clay dolls into a river. The dolls are surrogates for the human sacrifices once offered to the Ganges River. At first, the substitutes were life-sized but gradually shrunk to the size of dolls. (When the Nile River didn't rise on time, it received the same "gift" of children thrown into it in supplication. Eventually, the ancient Egyptians substituted dolls made of reeds or straw.)

Mummiform dolls called Ushabti were placed in ancient Egyptian tombs. Historians believe they represented the servants who, in their time, would have been buried alive with their deceased masters to work in the afterlife. Ushabtis also answered for any actions the deceased had taken while alive, hence the origin of the name, which means "one that answers." Ushabtis varied considerably in size and material, depending upon the wealth of the deceased. They were usually molded out of faience, a paste made of ground quartz or sand with a high percentage of quartz, although some were made of terra cotta, wood, or stone.

Basic Pattern for
STRENGTH

FOR WOVEN CLOTH

PREPARING THE PATTERN PIECES

1. Cut out the photocopied pattern pieces.

2. Place the body pattern piece on a double layer of fabric, right sides together. Pin the pattern in place. Trace the pattern with a soft lead pencil or disappearing fabric marker. Remove the pattern from the fabric.

3. Cut out the body fabric. Baste it together, with the right sides together.

ASSEMBLING THE DOLL

4. Machine-stitch on the marked line from near the center of the head to the bottom of the body on each side, backstitching at the beginning and at the end. Leave the top half of the head and the bottom open. Trim to $1/8$ inch (3 mm) from the seams. Trim to $1/2$ inch (1.3 cm) from the line on the top half of the head and the bottom. Apply seam sealant to these openings if needed.

5. Finger-fold a hem on the top half of the head and at the base of the doll. Fold the hem exactly on the stitching line. Pin the hem in place, and then baste. Remove the pins, clip the curves, and turn the fabric right side out.

6. Firmly stuff the arms and body up to the neck.

FASHIONING THE MASK

7. Place the mask pattern on a double thickness of fabric, right sides together. Trace around the pattern with a soft lead pencil or disappearing fabric marker. Baste the fabric layers together; then machine-stitch all the way around the line. Trim to $1/8$ inch (3 mm) from the seam. Clip the curves.

8. On one layer of fabric only, cut a $1 1/2$-inch (3.8 cm) slit straight across the middle of the mask forehead. Turn the mask right side out through this opening, and smooth the seam from the inside. Baste the mask to the front of the doll's head, placing the side with the slit against the head so it's not visible.

FINISHING THE HEAD

9. Place the cardboard head armature into the head. Glue the cardboard to the inside of the back of the head if this can be done without the glue bleeding through the fabric.

10. Stuff the neck and head. Sew the top of the head closed, catching all layers of fabric, then remove the basting stitches.

BONDING & INSERTING THE BASE CARDBOARD

11. Glue the two 1-inch (2.5 cm) cardboard circles together. Apply glue to the top surface of the stacked circles, and press them up into the bottom of the body. (The glue will adhere to the stuffing.)

12. Glue together the two 3-inch (7.6 cm) cardboard circles.

MAKING THE BASE FABRIC

13. Place the base pattern on doubled fabric, right sides together, and trace it with a soft lead pencil or disappearing fabric marker. Machine-stitch on the line around one-half of the circle, backstitching at the beginning and end. Trim the seam allowance, clip the curves, and turn the fabric right side out. Turn the open fabric edges to the inside exactly on the marked line. Baste this hem in place, making a smooth curve.

ATTACHING THE BODY
TO THE BASE FABRIC

14. Evenly spread glue on the bottom side of the small stacked cardboard piece that is in the base of the body. Place the body on the center of the base, and sew it to the top layer of the base fabric.

FINISHING THE BASE

15. Evenly spread glue over both sides of the 3-inch (7.6 cm) base armature cardboard circle. Insert the cardboard into the base fabric and push it into place. Pin the open sides closed. Press the base fabric to the cardboard until the glue adheres, holding the body firmly against the base. When the glue is set, use a ladder stitch to sew the base opening shut.

FOR NONWOVEN CLOTH

PREPARING THE PATTERN PIECES

1. Cut out the photocopied pattern pieces. Pin or baste them to the fabric and trace. Remove the pattern pieces. Cut out the fabric shapes on the marked lines.

2. Trace the armature pattern pieces onto the cardboard, and cut out on the marked lines.

ASSEMBLING THE DOLL

3. Baste the mask to the top of the body piece.

4. Apply a very thin layer of glue to the back of the cardboard head insert. On the inside of the rear body piece, center the cardboard over the head and press it down.

5. Baste the front and the rear body pieces together. Start at the bottom of the body, and sew up one side of the doll. When you've sewn almost around the head, pause and gently stuff the head, and then continue sewing. When you've sewn to 1/2 inch (1.3 cm) below the second arm, pause and firmly stuff the arms and neck. Continue sewing until you reach the bottom of the doll. Leave the bottom open.

JOINING THE DOLL TO THE BASE

6. Apply glue to both sides of the 1-inch (2.5 cm) cardboard circle. Insert it into the very bottom of the doll body. Immediately place the doll onto the center of the top circle of base-felt. Pin the doll in place; then sew the body and the base-felt together.

7. Apply glue to one side of the 3-inch (7.6 cm) cardboard base insert. Affix the cardboard in the center of the bottom piece of base-felt.

8. Apply glue to the top side of the 3-inch (7.6 cm) cardboard base insert. Place the top piece of the base-felt (with the doll attached) on top of the cardboard, and smooth the felt. A good bond between these pieces provides a stable base for the doll.

9. When all the glue is dry, sew the base fabric layers together using a decorative stitch.

Pamela Hastings'
STRENGTH

This totemic figure has a wise demeanor. Perhaps he's a tribal prophet, healer, or judge. The texture of the synthetic suede makes a fitting skin. Bright primary accent fabrics and beads enhance its native design.

PREPARING THE PATTERN PIECES

1. Cut out the photocopied patterns. Trace the body pattern onto the right side of the synthetic suede with a fine-tip permanent marker. Do not cut out.

2. Trace the decorative pattern pieces onto the wrong side of the other colors of synthetic suede, and cut out. Trace the head and base armature patterns onto cardboard, and cut out.

what you need

Basic sewing kit

Photocopied doll patterns, pages 142-143

Two 6 x 11-inch (15.2 x 27.9 cm) pieces of synthetic suede for body

4 small pieces of synthetic suede, assorted colors

Lightweight cardboard for armature

Fabric glue

Heavy object to weight the base (a stone or spent battery), less than 1 1/2 inches (3.8 cm) in any dimension, as dense as possible.

4 white disk beads, 1/2 inch (1.3 cm) in diameter

11 dark disk beads, 1/4 inch (6 mm) in diameter

Assorted pony beads

Assorted seed beads

Red cylinder bead, 3/4 inch (1.9 cm) long

ATTACHING THE APPLIQUES

3. Place the decorative synthetic suede pieces for the lower torso (1) and the lower face (2) onto the right side of the body. Hold them in place with a few drops of white glue.

4. Using a contrasting color thread, carefully sew around the very edges of the lower torso (1) and the lower face (2) pieces. Once you've completed the edging, add some decorative topstitching.

5. Position the six 1/2 x 1-inch (1.3 x 2.5 cm) synthetic suede strips (3) on the torso. Glue them in place. Glue the large piece (4) of synthetic suede to the torso. (It will cover the ends of the strips in the center of the torso.)

6. Place the synthetic suede mask (5) and arm strips (6). Carefully lift one end of the piece at a time to glue.

7. Stitch all the decorative synthetic suede pieces in place, sewing close to their outside edges.

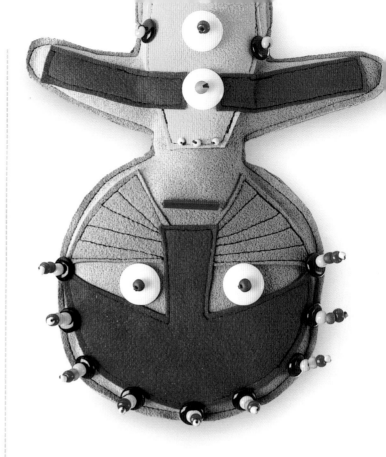

ASSEMBLING THE DOLL

8. With their wrong sides together, place the decorated front body fabric pieces on top of the plain 6 x 11-inch (15.2 x 27.9 cm) piece of synthetic suede. Put the cardboard head armature between the two synthetic suede body pieces.

9. To hold the body pieces in place, pin the synthetic suede together outside the marked pattern line. Carefully topstitch 1/8 inch (3 mm) inside the drawn line, leaving the bottom of the figure open.

10. Trim both pieces of the body inside the drawn line so the mark is cut away.

STUFFING & WEIGHTING THE DOLL

11. First stuff the doll gently in the head, then firmly in the arms and neck. Stop stuffing 2 inches (5 cm) from the bottom opening.

12. Wrap the heavy weight in stuffing so it won't dent the body. Insert the wrapped weight into the base of the doll. Stuff around the weight until the body is nicely filled.

CONSTRUCTING THE BASE

13. Trace the base pattern onto the wrong side of the bottom synthetic suede layer with a fine-tip permanent marker. Do not cut out. Glue the base cardboard in the center of the marked circle. Let dry.

14. Trace the base pattern onto the right side of the top synthetic suede layer with a fine-tip permanent marker. Do not cut out. Place the wrong side of the top base layer of synthetic suede over the cardboard.

15. Pin the base synthetic suede together outside the marked pattern line. Carefully topstitch $^1/_8$ inch (3 mm) inside the drawn line. Trim both pieces of the base fabric inside the drawn line so the mark is cut away.

16. Glue the wrong side of the 1$^1/_2$-inch synthetic suede decorative base piece to the center of the top of the base.

CONNECTING THE DOLL TO THE BASE

17. Apply glue to both sides of the 1-inch (2.5 cm) cardboard armature. Insert it into the very bottom of the doll body. Immediately place the doll onto the center of the base. Pin the doll in place; then sew the body and the base together. Let dry.

EMBELLISHING WITH BEADS

18. Sew a single contrasting color of seed beads around the bottom of the doll's body where it meets the base. Also attach a row of these beads to the top of pattern piece 4.

19. Create the eyes and central torso embellishments by combining a white disc bead, $^1/_2$ inch (1.3 cm) in diameter, with a colorful pony bead. Stack three pony beads on top of a dark disk bead to make the hair. Secure the top of each strand with a seed bead.

20. To make a breast, stack one pony bead on top of a dark disk bead, and sew it to the torso; repeat for the other breast. Use the cylinder bead to make the mouth. Sew it under the mask.

DOLLS *for* Good Luck

Dolls have played a central role in promoting good luck. Many figurative symbols and related rituals have evolved to encourage health, wealth, and a bountiful harvest.

In ancient China, every house had a small shrine of carved soapstone dolls representing deities. People gave gifts to the dolls, believing they'd gain wealth and fortune for themselves. Although the figures were originally revered as gods, over time they became amulets and good-luck symbols.

The wooden Lent dolls of Sorrento, Italy, hang in hotels after Ash Wednesday. Their feet are attached to a wooden ball, apple, or orange; one white and six black feathers protrude, pointing downward. The black feathers represent the six weeks of Lent, the period of fasting and penitence that precedes Easter. One feather is pulled out each week, and on Easter Sunday the white feather is removed. As the feathers are plucked out, they are burned for good luck.

The Inuit made dolls with faces carved from walrus tusks, reindeer horn, bone, or driftwood. Their bodies were dressed in animal skin. Often, the Inuit took good-luck dolls on fishing expeditions, tying them to the kayak for protection.

Some African tribes believe that harm befalls the owner of a doll that suffers damage. In case of fires or other emergencies, dolls are the first items rescued from their homes. A tribe in the Ivory Coast uses dolls to drive witches away. But not all witches are considered bad: the Norwegian kitchen witch doll looks after the welfare of the family. Hanging high from a string, she rides her broomstick, making sure that toast doesn't burn, cakes don't fall, and puddings don't boil over.

The Otomi Indians of Mexico make paper idols for their "seed baptism" crop ceremonies. The dolls, their arms raised in supplication, have corn, peanuts, peppers, or sugarcane sprouting from their legs and arms. To ensure a good crop yield, the paper doll is dipped into the blood of a sacrificed animal, then buried in the field.

Lynne Sward's
STRENGTH

Dark and light, soft and hard, matte and shiny—this portrayal of Strength features contrasting elements working together in complete harmony. You'll enjoy learning and using the fringe technique to great effect. Embossing copper foiling is another bright idea.

FORMING THE FOUNDATION

1. Use sharp scissors to cut the correct length of pipe foam insulation. Make your cut as even as possible. Spread the foam apart where it splits for an easier cut.

FASHIONING THE FRINGE SKIRT

2. Measure, mark, and cut a 9¹/₂ x 7-inch (24.1 x 17.8 cm) rectangle out of the cotton skirt fabric.

3. Using a rotary cutter, make 12 to 14 horizontal strips of the skirt fringe fabric. Each strip should be 3 x 6 inches (7.6 x 15.2 cm).

4. Double the fringe fabric, wrong sides together. Sew the doubled strips together about ¹/₈ inch (3 mm) from one edge.

5. Use a rotary cutter to make cuts ¹/₄-inch (6 mm) apart into the strips formed in step 4. Cut to below the stitching line from the bottom to the top of the strip.

6. Center the fringed strips in the middle of the fabric rectangle cut in step 2. There should be a ¹/₂-inch (1.3 cm) margin of foundation fabric on either side of the fringe.

7. Pin a fringe strip in place 3¹/₂ inches (8.9 cm) up from the bottom of the foundation fabric. Attach the strip using a straight stitch. Layer, pin, and sew the rest of the fringe strips onto the foundation fabric.

8. Wet the fringed rectangle under running water. Wring the fabric to remove most of the moisture. Dry the rectangle in a clothes dryer for approximately 15 minutes. (Let the fabric air-dry completely if it's still damp after being removed from the dryer.) The fringe will fluff up and look irregular.

SEWING ON THE SKIRT

9. Pin the fringed fabric onto the foam cylinder. Turn in one raw edge on the back of the fabric, and slip-stitch it to the other edge. Turn under the top and bottom fabric edges, and sew them in place.

PREPARING THE BODY FABRIC

10. Use the basic photocopied pattern only for the neck, arms, and upper torso. Cut out the abbreviated pattern. Place it onto the upper body fabric, doubled, with its right sides together. Pin the pattern in place. Trace the pattern with a soft lead pencil or disappearing fabric marker. Remove the pattern from the fabric.

11. Cut out the body fabric. Baste it together, right sides facing.

SEWING & STUFFING THE BODY FABRIC

12. Machine-stitch on the marked line from a point near the side of the neck to slightly under the arms on each side, backstitching at the beginning and at the end. Leave the neck and the torso open. Trim to $^1/_8$ inch (3 mm) from the seams. Trim to $^1/_2$ inch (1.3 cm) from the line at the openings. Apply seam sealant to these openings if needed.

13. Finger-fold a hem on the line at both openings. Pin the hem in place, then baste. Remove the pins, clip the curves; then turn the fabric right side out.

14. Stuff the neck and torso, and fit it over the fringed section at the top of the foam tube. Pin in place.

FINISHING THE SKIRT

15. Make one strip of the torso fabric, and fringe it completely, following the directions in steps 3 through 5. Attach the fringe strip to the bodice and hand-sew it in place.

WEIGHTING & FINISHING THE BASE

16. Lightly stuff the bottom cavity of the doll, then insert the three coarse hex nuts and the hexcap. Turn any excess fabric on the bottom of the doll into the cavity.

17. Cut a $3^1/_2$-inch (8.9 cm) piece of skirt fabric into a circle. Sew a running stitch $^1/_4$ inch (6 mm) from the edge of the circle. Put the three fender washers into the middle of the circle. Gently pull the stitch to close the fabric around the washers.

18. Pin the fabric-covered washers to the bottom of the foam cylinder. Using extra-strong doubled thread and small overcast or slip stitches, sew the washer to the bottom of the cylinder along the edge. At the end, make a square knot; then cut and bury the thread.

CREATING THE FACE & HEAD

19. Draw a face on a piece of paper, or use the template on page 144. Lay the face over the piece of brass foil. Trace the drawing onto the foil with a ballpoint pen. Remove the drawing or template. Retrace the design with an embossing stylus. (This works best if you place the foil on a thick magazine.)

20. Make two circles for the head from the same fabric as the arms and chest. Sew the circles together, right sides facing.

21. Make a slit in the back of the sewn fabric circle. Turn, then press the fabric. Using a zigzag stitch, attach the foil face onto the front of the head.

ADDING THE FINAL TOUCHES

22. Sew a circle of seed beads and a few strands of bead fringe around the edge of the head, using a backstitch. Pin and hand-overcast stitch the face shape to the stuffed neck back.

23. Hand-sew beads randomly on the chest and arm area.

Barbara Evans'
STRENGTH

This elegant interpretation resembles a traditional African fertility doll. The complementary colors of the rust-colored felt and cobalt blue embroidery thread transform the primitive doll into a sophisticated figure. Multi-colored beads add just the right amount of flourish.

PREPARING THE PATTERN PIECES

1. Cut out all the photocopied pattern pieces, and trace them onto the back of the felt with a light pencil or erasable marking pen. Trace the body shape twice. Cut out the fabric on the marked line.

what you need

Basic sewing kit

Photocopied doll patterns, pages 141–142

Photocopied breast pattern, page 144

¹/₂ yard (45.7 cm) of felt for body, mask, chest, base, and armature

Embroidery threads

2 disk bead for eyes

Disk bead for mouth

Lightweight cardboard for armature

Fabric glue

Assorted beads for mask and jewelry

2. Cut out all the photocopied armature pattern pieces. Transfer them onto cardboard, and cut out on the marked line.

3. Baste the mask to the head at the top of the body piece.

DECORATING THE FACE

4. Embroider a decorative stitch pattern around the lower edge of the mask. Embroider a decorative stitch pattern around the top of the mask, ¹/₄ inch (6 mm) in from the edge. (Adjust this distance to accommodate the stitch you'll use to sew the body pieces together.)

5. Sew the eye beads and mouth bead onto the face as shown in figure 1. (You could embroider these two features.) Use other embroidery stitches (see pages 15 and 16) to make additional facial features or markings.

Figure 1

ASSEMBLING THE DOLL

6. Follow steps 4 and 5 of the basic pattern for Strength (nonwoven fabric) on page 62.

CREATING THE BREASTS

7. Embroider a decorative stitch around the outside edge of each breast. Sew a tiny seed bead in the center of each breast. Glue the breasts to the body.

JOINING THE DOLL TO THE BASE

8. Follow steps 6 through 9 of the basic pattern for Strength (nonwoven fabric) on page 62.

BEADING THE NECKLACES

9. Use a beading needle and thread to string about 25 inches (63.5 cm) of beads. Use a few larger beads to add weight to the chain. This will help stabilize the base. Wrap the bead strand around the doll's base. Knot and glue the bead thread before trimming.

10. String, and then sew three strands of assorted seed beads tightly around the doll's neck.

11. The two lower-hanging bead strands do not fully circle the neck. Anchor the bead thread at the side of the neck; then string the lower strand of beads. Put the needle back in on the opposite side of the neck, push it straight through, and bring it out where you started. Repeat this process for the second bead strand, and anchor the thread at the side of the neck.

BEADING THE CROWN OF THE HEAD

12. There are two ways to attach the beads to the crown of the head. The first method is to sew on each bead individually (see figure 2). Start in the center at the top of the head, and work down one side. Repeat the process on the opposite side of the head. The second method is to make one long bead strand, then attach it to the head by sewing a couching stitch between each bead. Securely anchor one end of the bead strand. Tie a temporary knot in the opposite end to hold the beads on while you couch the length of the strand. Securely anchor the second end of the strand.

Figure 2

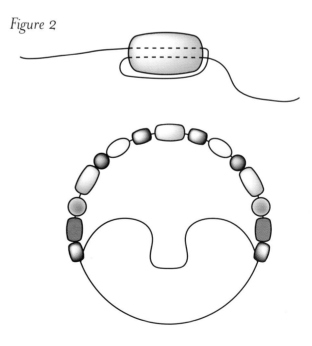

MAKING EARRINGS

13. Figure 3 shows how to make an earring. Go through a larger bead, then string enough seed beads to form a loop. Go back through the larger bead with your needle. Make an earring for each side of the head.

Figure 3

DOLLS *for* Magic

Beware of casually leaving your nail clippings or the hair you clean out of your brush in the trash; you might have an enemy versed in the art of making, or worse yet, using, voodoo dolls.

Hollywood receives some of the blame for misconceptions about voodoo, recognized today as a legitimate religion, and voodoo dolls—made of cloth, stuffed with herbs, personalized with something belonging to the intended victim, and bristling with pins. In reality, voodoo practitioners just as regularly use their dolls to direct healing energy. They often employ factory-made dolls, or at least use their components (such as heads), attached to decorated bottles. In other cases, the "dolls" have absolutely no human features, sometimes looking more like jugs.

The practice of piercing "spite" dolls with pins and nails has existed around the world for centuries. In England during the Middle Ages, a magician died in jail for making wax and canvas *poppets*, as they were called. In central India, wooden figures were pierced with nails to bring injury to an enemy. To wreak vengeance in China, one might dress a straw doll with a cotton head in blood-stained paper, and then pierce it with needles while making incantations. At the Temple of Unfortunate Women in Canton, wives wishing their husbands to reform would hang paper figures of men upside down.

Dolls also have been used for less nefarious purposes. For example, a girl wishing for a lover would make a wax doll and throw it in a fire to induce the object of her affection to melt with love for her. In witchcraft, love poppets ensure permanent and lasting love. Two poppets made from bedsheets, optimally, or cloth (preferably used by each member of the couple) are stuffed with sacred herbs while the maker chants the name of the person each effigy represents. Over an altar, the poppets are bound facing each other with red ribbon cut in a length divisible by seven.

Tracy Stilwell's
STRENGTH

The results you can get just by playing with the placement and size of facial features are amazing. This doll's wry sense of humor comes from just that. One paperclay eye is firmly fixed to the head, while one is suspended atop a copper wire spring. Talk about seeing things from a new perspective!

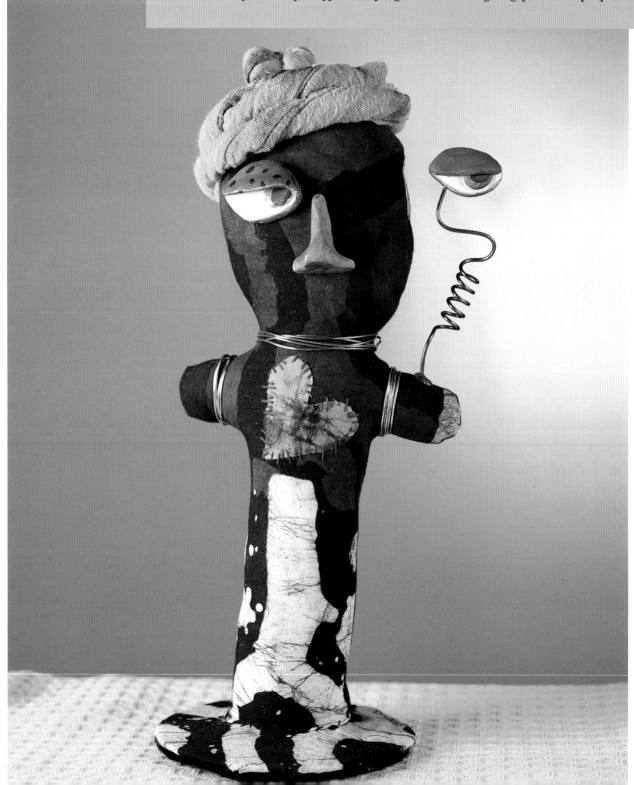

PREPARING THE PATTERN PIECES & ASSEMBLING THE DOLL

1. Follow steps 1 through 6 of the basic pattern for Strength (woven fabric) on page 61.

FINISHING THE HEAD

2. Follow steps 9 and 10 of the basic pattern for Strength (woven fabric).

CONSTRUCTING THE BASE & ATTACHING THE DOLL

3. Follow steps 11 through 15 of the basic pattern for Strength (woven fabric).

CREATING THE EYES & NOSE

4. Twist the copper wire around a thin dowel several times, leaving about 1 inch (2.5 cm) of straight wire at one end, and 2 inches (5 cm) at the other.

5. Read and follow the manufacturer's instructions for working with paperclay. Sculpt two eyes and a nose with the paperclay. While the clay is soft, stick the long end of the twisted copper wire into the corner of one clay eye. Let the sculpted features dry for the recommended time.

6. Tint the hardened paperclay with acrylic paints. Let dry. Glue the nose and wire-free eye in place on the face. Glue the stem of the copper wire that holds the second eye to the arm.

ADDING THE FINAL TOUCHES

7. Wrap the brass-colored wire around each arm and the neck several times, crossing in the back as needed.

8. Tightly twist the turban fabric. Wrap it onto the top of the head, arranging it in an attractive fashion. Hand-stitch the turban in place.

9. Cut a heart-shaped applique out of the patterned fabric. Stitch it to the front of the body with embroidery thread.

Arlinka Blair's
STRENGTH

This doll's unique personality comes from its irresistible nubby textures, attractive earth-tone palette, and casual wrap styling. It serves as a fantastic reminder to keep the figure loose to allow its character to emerge during the creative process.

PREPARING THE PATTERN PIECES & ASSEMBLING THE DOLL

1. Follow steps 1 through 6 of the basic pattern for Strength (woven cloth) on page 61.

FASHIONING THE MASK

2. Place the mask pattern onto doubled mask fabric, right sides together. Trace the pattern with a soft lead pencil or disappearing fabric marker. Baste the fabric layers together; then machine-stitch completely around the mask on the line. Trim to $^1/_8$ inch (3 mm) from the seam. Clip the curves.

3. Cut a $^1/_2$-inch (3.8 cm) slit straight across the middle of one layer of the mask fabric. Turn the mask right side out through this opening, and smooth the seam from the inside. Slightly stuff the mask. Baste the mask to the front of the head, placing the slit fabric against the head so it's not visible.

COMPLETING THE BASIC DOLL FORM

4. Follow steps 9 through 15 of the basic pattern for Strength (woven cloth).

WRAPPING THE DOLL

5. Wrap the doll's torso with the distressed fabric starting under its arms and moving to the base. Fray the edges of the fabric. With an embroidery needle and thread, securely stitch the wrapped torso fabric to the doll body, encircling the torso with random decorative stitches.

6. Wrap the thick textured fabric strip around the bottom of the doll's torso where it meets the base. Circle the doll two or three times. Use a strong fabric glue to adhere the end of the wrapped fabric at the back of the doll. (This thick wrap helps the doll stand upright.)

7. Cut a narrow strip of the base wrap fabric. Cross this fabric over and under the figure's arms, making an X on the front of the doll. Tie the ends of the strip together in the back of the doll.

CREATING THE FACE

8. Securely attach the bottle-cap mouth at the base of the head with embroidery thread.

9. Sew one button eye onto the face under each arch of the mask.

APPLYING DECORATIVE ACCENTS

10. Attach the milagros or charms with embroidery thread. Sew one milagro at the end of each arm, one on either side of the mouth, and one at the top of the torso wrap.

11. Use embroidery threads in coordinating colors to make a single row of fringe across the top seam of the head from eye level to eye level. To make the fringe, insert the needle just below the seam on one side of the head, and gently pull it through. Leave at least 2 inches (5 cm) of thread trailing the insertion. Loop the needle back over the seam and re-insert it near the original piercing. Tightly pull the thread through to the other side. Clip the thread to the desired length.

12. Make more fringe to hang from the bottom of the face like whiskers. Embellish the mask, the sides of the face, and the shoulders with more decorative stitching as desired.

what you need

Basic sewing kit

Photocopied doll patterns, pages 141–142

$^1/_2$ yard (45.7 cm) of thin-textured fabric (such as terrycloth) for body and base

6 x 6-inch (15.2 x 15.2 cm) piece of printed fabric for mask

Light cardboard for armature

Fabric glue

Long narrow scrap of distressed fabric (such as denim or linen) for body wrap

Thick textured scrap of fabric (such as fleece) for base wrap

Bottle cap

Embroidery threads

2 buttons for eyes

5 milagros or charms

Unique Pattern
PROJECTS

To show the expressive energy of dollmaking, we invited 10 talented
designers to create one-of-a-kind patterns. By making their dolls,
you'll sharpen your skills and learn many more imaginative techniques.
Whether you're tinting cloth, tooling a face, or fringing hair, you're
sure to enjoy a unique dollmaking adventure.

Pamela Hastings
STICK GUY

Isn't this suave hipster the life of the party? Fabric selection is crucial to creating such sophisticated attire, so look for scraps with extra appeal. You can use your best beads here; they'll get plenty of notice. So will the artfully raised eyebrow—such a little detail can really add style.

CREATING THE FABRIC BODY

1. Cut out the photocopied pattern pieces. Trace the body pattern onto the body fabric twice. Cut out the two body pieces.

2. With the right sides of the fabric together, sew across the shoulders from A to B. Iron the fabric. Clip the sewn curves. Turn the fabric and press again. (Frequent pressing makes small fabric pieces crisp.)

SEWING THE SMALL FABRIC ELEMENTS

3. Trace each of the six small pattern elements onto the wrong sides of each of the six cotton fabrics. Do not cut out the pieces.

4. Double the fabric with the right sides together. Pin and stitch $1/8$ inch (3 mm) inside the outline, leaving openings as indicated. Press, and then clip the fabric.

5. Turn the fabric right side out. Turn in the raw fabric edges, and slip-stitch the openings to close.

ATTACHING THE SMALL FABRIC ELEMENTS TO THE BODY

6. Pile the decorative fabric sections on the front of the body, and pin them in place. Using two colors of heavy thread and a running stitch, sew along the edge of the top fabric section, going through all three decorative pieces and the front body fabric.

BEADING THE SMALL FABRIC ELEMENTS

7. Decorate the two stacked medallions with beads. On this doll, the top section has three bead strands, and the bottom area has a single large bead.

SECURING THE BODY TO THE STICK

8. Drape the body fabric over the stick with the wrong sides together. Match the edges, and pin the fabric in place. Use a running stitch with the two colors of heavy thread to sew the back to the front, $1/4$ inch (6 mm) in from the edge. Insert a little stuffing between the two layers of fabric to fill it out. Make parallel stitches at the bottom of the legs if you wish.

BEADING THE BODY FABRIC

9. Work strands of beads into the stitching as desired. (When the artist started or ended a new piece of thread, she made a double knot, and added a few beads.) Make a few stitches around the stick at each wrist to anchor the stick.

CREATING THE HEAD

10. Trace the head-pattern piece onto the osnaburg or muslin. Lightly trace the facial features onto the opposite side with a pencil.

11. With the right sides of the fabric together, match the head to a scrap of the body material. Pin these elements together, and sew them $1/4$ inch (6 mm) inside the marked line. Leave the top of the head open.

12. Iron, and then clip the sewn head. Turn the fabric right side out, and stuff it, keeping the head somewhat flat, but nicely filled. Pin, and then slip-stitch the top edges of the head together, turning the front edge under and overlapping the back.

DRAWING THE FACE

13. Draw the main lines of the facial features in a wide-tip permanent marker. Use colored pencils for shading.

MAKING THE HAIR

14. Using the two colors of heavy thread, make a triple knot, add three pony beads, and sew this accent into the top left corner of the head. Stitch through the top of the head, adding seven pony beads to each stitch, and going through the same side of the head each time (see figure 1). Work the loops across the top of the head. End by going out the top right corner of the head, adding three pony beads, and tying a triple knot as close to the beads as possible. Cut off the thread, leaving a 1-inch (2.5 cm) tail.

COMPLETING THE DOLL

15. Using the same two colors of heavy thread and a ladder stitch, attach the head to the body at the neck. With the same thread, sew a loop to the center back of the head for hanging. (This doll is light enough to be hung on the wall with the loop over a pushpin.)

Figure 1

Beth Carter
WILY WOMAN

This wily woman is chock full of moxie. With her oversized stretched-out hands, she really embraces life. The simple bent-wire frame is a breeze to make, and you'll love styling her whimsical wardrobe of mix-and-match fabrics.

SEWING THE BODY FABRIC

1. Double the body fabric lengthwise, right sides together. Sew up the long side, leaving a $^1/_4$-inch (6 mm) seam. Turn the fabric right side out.

BENDING THE WIRE FOR THE TOP OF THE HEAD

2. Fold the galvanized steel wire in half. This is the center knob of the head. From the top of the knob, measure down $^1/_4$ to $^1/_2$ inch (6 mm to 1.3 cm). Bend the wire up at this point with the round-nose pliers. Make this bend on both sides of the center knob as shown in figure 1.

3. Bend the wire back down to create two more knobs, one on each side of the center knob.

BENDING THE WIRE & ATTACHING BEAD EYES

4. Measure $^1/_2$ inch (1.3 cm) down from the top of one outside knob, and bend the wire in toward the center of the face (see figure 2). Place the round-nose pliers $^1/_2$ inch (1.3 cm) down from the bend. Thread an eye bead onto the wire until it's stopped by the pliers. Keeping the bead against the pliers, pull the tail of the wire around like a hand on a clock (see figure 3) to create the eye loop and secure the bead.

5. Repeat step 4 make a second eye on the opposite side of the face.

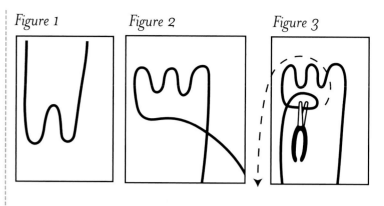

Figure 1   Figure 2   Figure 3

TWISTING THE WIRE FOR THE NECK & BODY

6. Bring both sides of the wire together at the neck, and begin twisting them to form the neck and body. Twist 3 inches (7.6 cm) of wire for the body as shown in figure 4. At the bottom of the body is the hip point.

ADDING THE MUSLIN & BODY FABRIC

7. Wrap the muslin around the body, leaving a $^1/_4$-inch (6 mm) gap below the neck and above the hip. Pull the body fabric tube over the muslin up to the neck.

MAKING THE LEGS, ANKLES & TOES

8. At the hip point, separate the ends of the wire to form the legs. Measure 2 inches (5 cm) down the leg wires, and make a 90° angle bend in each wire to create ankles (see figure 5).

9. Face the doll toward you to form its toes. Place the round-nose pliers approximately 1 inch (2.5 cm) down from one ankle, and bend the wire away from you. Place the pliers $^1/_2$ inch (1.3 cm) down the wire from the top of the "big toe," and bend the wire back toward you. Continue this bending pattern to form all five toes on one foot. (Placing the pliers closer to or further away from the last bend varies the toe size.) After making the last toe, bend the wire back to the ankle. Wrap the wire around the ankle once to secure. Reshape the toes and foot as desired.

10. Spread the doll's legs. Holding the foot securely in one hand and the wire's end in the other, begin wrapping the wire up the doll's leg. (By holding the wire on the end you'll create a more open leg wrap.) Continue wrapping up the leg and body until you run out of wire (see figure 6).

Figure 4 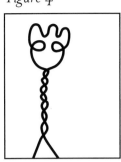   *Figure 5*    *Figure 6* 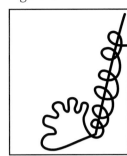   *Figure 7*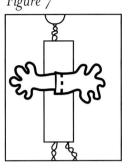

11. With the doll facing you, repeat steps 9 and 10 to make the second foot and leg wrap.

FINISHING THE BODY

12. If needed, reshape the doll's armature so it stands upright on your work surface. The doll's body fabric should fall just below the hip bend and cover where you finished wrapping the legs with wire.

13. Fill the body fabric with polyester stuffing to the desired fullness, leaving a $1/4$-inch (6 mm) fabric margin at the top and bottom. To finish the neck, hold the front and back of the fabric together, and stitch closed with seed beads. At the bottom opening, place a small amount of glue under the fabric and onto the stuffing to secure.

CREATING & ATTACHING THE HANDS

14. Cut out the photocopied hand pattern. Place it onto doubled hand fabric, right sides together. Trace the pattern onto the fabric, and sew on the line. Cut out the hands, leaving a $1/4$-inch (6 mm) seam. Clip the curves between the fingers, and turn the fabric.

15. Stuff the hands; then bead or embellish them as you wish. Turn the seams at the wrists, and stitch closed.

16. Pin the hands on the back of the doll. Sew the hands into place by stitching through the body fabric and the muslin several times to secure (see figure 7). If the hands flop backwards, stitch further up through the wrist and into the body of the doll.

EMBELLISHING THE DOLL

17. Pin the fringe to the bottom of the body fabric, and stitch in place. String the necklace beads on the waxed linen. Add other embellishments as desired. Reshape the doll to be freestanding.

Front view of alternate doll design

Rear view of alternate doll design

Lynne Sward
PERSONAL SYMBOL FIGURE

Feel free to develop your own unique silhouette for this doll. You'll also have the opportunity to design your own fabric and embellish the doll in any imaginable way. Does this sound too good to be true? That's the essence of creating a personal symbol figure.

ATTACHING THE DECORATIVE FABRIC APPLIQUE

1. Arrange and machine-stitch the interesting fabric scraps onto the foundation fabric. Further embellish the surface with additional machine-stitching.

CREATING THE DOLL BODY

2. On paper, draw a simple doll body silhouette from toe to neck. Cut out the paper figure, and pin it to the finished fabric. Cut out the fabric following the contour of the paper pattern.

3. Pin the wrong sides of the body fabric together. Hand-sew the front to the back using a short-width satin stitch around all the edges. Leave the neck area open.

4. Stuff the body figure as firmly and as evenly as you can. Hand-sew the neck closed, using an overcast stitch.

what you need

Basic sewing kit

Commercial fabric, twice the size of the doll body you wish to make

Interesting fabric scraps

Fabric interfacing, small piece

Glass, seed, and other decorative beads

Rotary cutter

Large accent bead

FORMING THE FACE

5. Cut two round face shapes out of fabric. Iron interfacing on the back of one of the shapes.

6. Cut out small fabric shapes to form the doll's facial features, such as its eyes, nose, and mouth. Satin-stitch the fabric features onto the face shape that has the interfacing. Further embellish the face with back-stitch bead embroidery.

STYLING THE HAIR

7. To make the hair, cut strips of coordinating fabrics. Layer two strips, wrong sides together, and sew down the center. Cut into the strips with a rotary cutter, above and below the stitching line.

8. Wet the fabric fringe strips under running water. Wring them to remove most of the moisture, and then dry them in a clothes dryer for approximately 15 minutes. (Let the fabric air-dry completely if it's still damp after being removed from the dryer.) The hair fringe will fluff up and look irregular.

FINISHING THE DOLL

9. Slip the hair fringe between the two face shapes. Hand-sew the face shapes together, securing the hair, and attaching the face at the neck of the doll.

10. Sew a large accent bead, such as a turquoise disk, and bead fringe onto the doll's chest for extra embellishment.

Pamela Hastings
FOLK ART DOLLS

The less perfect these dolls are, the more they resemble authentic folk art. Since they are quick to make, you can easily create a grouping of dolls in various sizes. This is a good pattern to use for a children's project. You also could tea-dye the body fabric for an aged appearance.

PREPARING THE PATTERN PIECES

1. Cut out the photocopied pattern pieces. Trace the patterns onto heavy paper or cardboard, and then cut out.

2. Fold the fabric right sides together, and iron flat if needed. Trace the body pattern onto the fabric with a soft pencil or erasable pen. Following traced lines, pin the folded cloth together. Cut out the cloth bodies.

3. Trace the fabric base patterns onto the wrong side of a single layer of fabric, and cut them out.

4. Cut out the photocopied pattern for the cardboard base. Trace it onto a sheet of cardboard, and then cut out outside the line.

ADHERING THE CARDBOARD BASE

5. Cover one side of the cardboard base with an even layer of white glue. Stick the base to another piece of cardboard. Place a weight on top of the glued, double-layered cardboard, and let dry.

SEWING THE BODY FABRIC

6. Before sewing the body parts together, finish any planned piecing or applique. If you doubt your face-drawing skills, lightly trace the features with a pencil on the front fabric at this time. Sew the two body shapes together, right sides facing, and leave their bottom edges open.

7. Fold the body in half. Clip a tiny V on the open edges at the center front and center back. Clip or mark the fabric base at points A and B to indicate the center front and center back. With the right sides together, sew the body to the base from A to B, matching the clips at the centers.

FILLING & CLOSING THE BODY FABRIC

8. Turn the fabric, and firmly stuff to within 3 inches (7.6 cm) of the base. Wrap the heavy weight in stuffing so it won't dent the body. Insert the wrapped weight into the base of the doll. Stuff around the weight until the body is nicely filled.

9. Cut out the double cardboard base. Insert the cardboard base into the base of the doll. Apply pressure if needed to mold the doll into an upright position. Pin-shut the opening at the back of the base; then slip-stitch closed.

PAINTING THE DOLL

10. Draw the lines and features on the doll with a light-colored pencil. Paint the doll body, filling in the lightest colors first. Let each color dry before painting next to it, unless you want the colors to slightly run.

11. Practice your face-painting technique on a scrap of the same fabric before working on the doll. When the face paint is dry, draw and shade the features with colored pencil. Use fine-tip markers to highlight features as desired.

TINTING THE PAINTED DOLL

12. Tint some acrylic gel medium with copper or gold acrylic paint. This finish ages the doll. Test the tinted gel on a sample of the painted fabric before using it on the doll. (If the tint is too dark, the facial features will disappear. If the tint is too light, apply another coat.) When the tint is ready and the painted doll is completely dry, brush the gel over the whole body. The gel will look white when applied, but dry clear.

Barbara Carleton Evans
DON'T CALL ME A SQUARE

This brightly clad and bejeweled goddess conceals her humble beginnings. Formed from two equally sized squares of cloth, she is based on the traditional "napkin" doll design. A single wire supports the head and hand beads. Choose fanciful fabrics and shiny beads to dazzle and delight.

SEWING & FOLDING THE BODY FABRIC

1. Apply any extra surface design techniques now while the body fabric is still a flat square.

2. Pin or baste the body fabric squares together, right sides facing. Machine-stitch around the outside edge leaving a $1/8$-inch (3 mm) seam. Leave a 4-inch (10.2 cm) opening in the center of one side. Clip the corners.

3. Turn the fabric right side out. Push all four corners out square. Hand-sew the opening closed; then iron the body fabric.

4. Fold the body as shown in figure 1. Tack the fabric so the folded points stay in place.

5. Gather the center 6 inches (15.2 cm) of fabric as shown in figure 2. Pull the gathering thread until the gathered fabric is 3 inches (7.6 cm) long.

PAINTING THE WOODEN BEADS

6. Paint the head and hand beads with two coats of acrylic paint and a finishing coat of matte varnish. An easy way to hold a bead while you paint it is to push the bead onto the end of a bent wire or pipe cleaner (figure 3). Hold the wire or pipe cleaner while you paint. Push the free wire end into a piece of foam to hold the wire and bead while the paint dries.

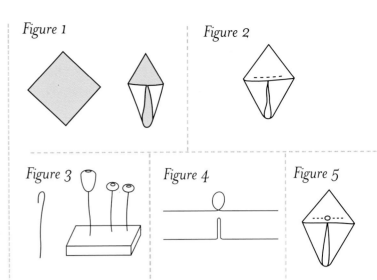

Figure 1

Figure 2

Figure 3

Figure 4

Figure 5

CREATING THE ARMS & NECK

7. Bend the telephone wire as shown in figure 4. Bend the neck loop in the center of the wire. Use a large needle or awl to make a hole in the body fabric at the point indicated in figure 5. Tightly pinch the neck loop and push it up through the fabric (figure 6). Open the loop a little, then push the head bead onto the wire (figure 7).

8. Make U-shape bends at both ends of the arm wire as shown in figure 8. Place a hand bead over each U-shape bend (see figure 9). Trim the wire if needed so the hands are just at the edge of the fabric fold as shown. Tack the fabric together at the wrists to hide the wire. Tack down the front triangle of fabric.

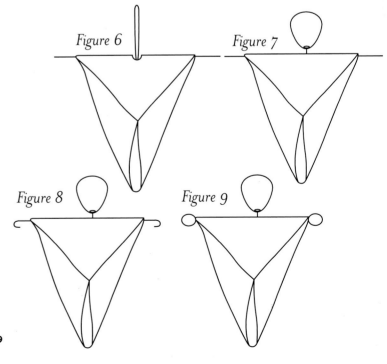

Figure 6

Figure 7

Figure 8

Figure 9

BEADING THE FABRIC

9. Add any beads not attached while the fabric was flat. Frequently backstitch to hold the beads securely. When making a row of seed beads only, backstitch every few beads. Figure 10 shows how to attach tubular beads. There is a seed bead between each tubular bead. Sew on charms, such as the moon faces, through their loops, then stitch twice across the neck of the loop to hold them securely (figure 11). For funnel beads, leave a little extra thread at the top so they swing. Since the funnel beads have large holes, they are strung as shown in figure 12, using a small glass heart bead inside the funnel bead and a seed bead at the end.

WRAPPING THE HEAD

10. If needed, hem the head-wrap fabric, or sew it into a tube. Play with the strip, wrapping it around the head bead in various ways until you achieve a pleasing arrangement. Pin the head wrap into place, then sew it together. Sew the head wrap to the body fabric at the base of the neck. Trim the end of the wrap, or tuck it into a fold. Embellish the wrap as desired.

CONSTRUCTING THE WINGS

11. Iron the bonding material to the wrong side of one piece of wing fabric. Discard the bonding material's protective paper. Fuse the second wing fabric piece to the first, wrong sides together.

12. Cut out the photocopied wing pattern, and lightly trace it onto the fabric. Cut out the fabric wing. Sew the wing to the back of the doll, adding beads where the wing is attached to the body.

Figure 10

Figure 11

Figure 12

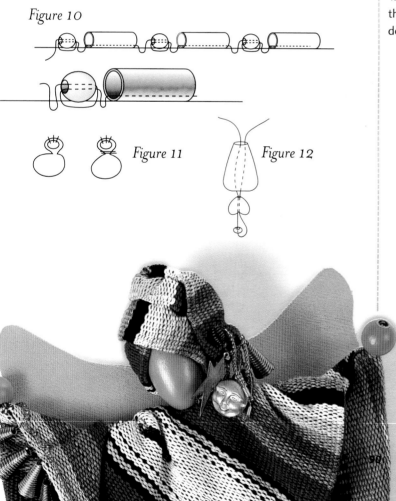

DOLLS
for
The Dead

In many cultures, dolls play an important role in rituals honoring the departed. Fashioning a likeness of the deceased can ease grief, celebrate life, and uphold a legacy.

Some African wood carvers make ancestral figures when someone dies, believing that the soul of the departed temporarily enters this figure before passing into the beyond. In this new dwelling place, the deceased watches over the fortunes of descendants and listens to their prayers.

If a child died, Ojibwa Indian women made a "doll of misfortune." Creating it from feathers and placing it in a cradle, the mother cared for the doll just as if it were a real baby. She would take it on journeys, talk to it, and give it presents for one year, until she considered the baby old enough to reach paradise on its own.

On the first and second days of November, Mexicans celebrate the Day of the Dead. They believe that on this day the deceased receive celestial permission to visit friends and relatives on earth. Although it sounds somber, this feast, which has regional differences in custom but is unique to Mexico, is actually one of the gayest holidays of the year, as the people socialize and celebrate the life of the departed. To welcome the dead, they spruce up grave sites, keep vigil in cemeteries, and set up special altars in their homes where they place offerings of food and drink. With a macabre sense of humor, the Mexican people decorate their homes with skeleton dolls and other toys. Craftspeople use wood, tin, papier-mâché, and clay to make these grimly funny figures. Many skeletons are portrayed in the midst of daily activities: children riding bicycles, musicians playing in a band, couples marrying in their wedding finery.

Lynne Sward
SEDONA SPIRIT

The flexible shape of the Sedona Spirit doll lets you create a meaningful and unique silhouette. Its foundation fabric of pieced scraps assures that no two dolls will ever be the same. This is a great doll to explore the connection between the figure and its message.

ATTACHING THE DECORATIVE FABRIC APPLIQUE

1. Arrange and machine-stitch the interesting fabric scraps onto the foundation fabric. Further embellish the surface with additional machine-stitching using metallic threads.

CREATING THE DOLL BODY

2. On paper, draw a simple doll body silhouette from toe to neck. Also draw a shape for the doll's head. Cut out the paper figures, and pin them to the finished fabric. Cut out the fabric, following the contour of the paper pattern.

3. Pin the wrong sides of the body fabric together. Hand-sew the front to the back using a short-width satin stitch around all the edges, leaving the neck area open.

4. Stuff the body figure as firmly and as evenly as you can. Hand-sew the neck closed, using an overcast stitch.

what you need

Basic sewing kit

Interesting fabric scraps

Foundation fabric, twice the size of the doll body you wish to make

Metallic threads

Permanent markers

Brass-tooling foil

Novelty yarns

ATTACHING THE FACE, HEAD & HAIR

5. Use permanent markers to draw a small face onto the brass-tooling foil. Cut out the foil around the face. Using a zigzag stitch, sew the foil onto the front of the head.

6. Place the two head pieces, wrong sides together, over the doll's neck. Hand-sew the edges of the head together. Cut pieces of coordinating novelty yarns and machine-stitch them at the top of the head.

Marcella Welch
NOMBLEH

In Xhosa, one of the 11 official languages of South Africa, Nombleh means beauty, a perfect name for this fantastic cloth doll. Nombleh is clothed in wonderfully simple-to-make clothing. Her hair is the perfect showplace for exotic yarns and threads.

SEWING THE BODY FABRIC

1. Transfer the photocopied pattern pieces to sturdy paper or poster board. Following the directional arrows, place the pattern pieces onto the cotton velour, and trace them on the wrong side of the doubled fabric. (Don't cut out the fabric as it's much easier to sew large pieces of velour.)

what you need

Basic sewing kit

Photocopied doll patterns, page 150

1/2 yard (45.7 cm) of cotton velour

Craft stick

2 yards (1.8 m) of colorful cotton for clothing

Assorted yarns, ribbons, and metallic threads for hair

Hot glue gun and glue stick

Pendants and beads for necklace and dress embellishment

2. Sew each pattern piece exactly on the trace-line. Cut out, using a 1/4-inch (6 mm) seam allowance. Turn all pattern pieces to the right side. Smooth the nap of the velour with your fingers.

STUFFING THE DOLL

3. Use a stuffing tool to push filler into the head. Shape the head with one hand as you firmly stuff with the other. Insert a craft stick into the neck for support as you stuff the neck area to approximately 1/2 inch (1.3 cm) from the opening.

4. Stuff the arms and legs, ending approximately 1/2 inch (1.3 cm) from their openings.

CLOSING & ATTACHING THE ARMS & LEGS

5. Match the front and back seam of the legs, turn in the raw edges, and then hand-sew closed with an overcast stitch. Hand-sew the rest of the body parts to close.

6. Hand-sew the arms and legs to the torso using an overcast stitch.

CREATING THE CAMISOLE

7. Cut a 10 x 8-inch (25.4 x 20.3 cm) piece of colorful fabric for the camisole. Make a 1/4-inch (6 mm) hem on the longest sides.

8. Place the fabric on the doll just underneath the arms, and sew it closed in the back. Sew the fabric taut at the top, allowing for more looseness toward the hips. Sew a couple of stitches between the doll's legs to form pants.

FORMING THE BODICE

9. Cut two 12 x 3-inch (30.5 x 7.6 cm) pieces of colorful fabric for the bodice of the dress. Sew a 1/4-inch (6 mm) hem on the long sides of each fabric piece.

10. Divide one piece of fabric in half, and place the center point on one shoulder of the doll. Repeat with the second fabric piece for the second shoulder. Cross one piece over the other at the waistline. Hand-stitch at the waist on both sides and where the fabric forms a V in the front and back.

FASHIONING THE SKIRT

11. Cut or tear three 4 x 45-inch (10.2 x 114.3 cm) strips of different fabrics. Sew the first strip to the second. Sew the third strip to the other two. With the right sides together, sew closed to form a skirt. Turn under a 1/4-inch (6 mm) hem on each raw edge. Press the skirt.

12. Hand-sew a gathering stitch around one edge of the skirt. Place the skirt on the doll at the waistline. Pull the thread taut to close around the waist. Knot the thread in the back of the skirt. Sew stitches through the skirt into the waistline to keep the skirt in place.

STYLING THE HAIR

13. Cut a piece of cardboard 3 inches (7.6 cm) wide. Assemble several different yarns, ribbons, and metallic threads. (For this doll, the artist used seven different yarns.) Wrap the yarns around the cardboard 30 times.

14. Cut one edge of the fiber loop and remove it from the cardboard. Carefully divide the yarn into 10 bundles. Tie each bundle at its center.

15. Starting at the top of the head, hot-glue or sew the first bundle onto the seam. Glue two more bundles onto the seam. Repeat for the other side of the head. Fill in the rest of the head with the remainder of the yarn bundles.

ACCESSORIZING
THE COSTUME

16. Thread a needle with quilting thread. Knot and attach the thread at the top of the doll's neck. String enough assorted beads and pendants to go around the doll's neck at least twice.

17. Repeat step 16 to make bracelets for the doll's wrists.

18. To make earrings, sew pendants or beads to the sides of the doll's face where ears would be positioned.

19. If you want Nombleh to hang on the wall, sew a cord to the back of her neck.

96

JoAnn Pinto
METAMORPHOSIS

Metamorphosis has cloth understructures with a stretch cotton knit overlay, or "skin," similar to a bodysuit or leotard. The space between the skin and the leotard is ideal for stuffing. It enables you to form subtle body curves that give the figure realism without adding darts or other complicated sewing techniques.

STANDARD SEWING DIRECTIONS

1. Cut out the photocopied pattern pieces. Trace the pattern pieces onto the fabric with a light pencil. Using a small stitch length, sew on the marked line. Trim the sewn pieces to an $^{1}/_{8}$-inch (3 mm) seam.

what you need

Basic sewing kit

Photocopied doll patterns, pages 151–152

$^{1}/_{2}$ yard (45.7 cm) of muslin or quilter's cloth for understructure

16-gauge wire for body

$^{1}/_{2}$ yard (45.7 cm) of four-way stretch cotton knit

22-gauge wire for hands

Needle-nose pliers

Transparent or floral tape

Hot glue gun and glue sticks

Scraps of coordinating fabric for costume

Glue stick

Assorted decorative threads and beads

Aluminum foil

Plastic wrap

Scrap paper

Glue or decoupage medium

Acrylic paint, tissue, or handmade paper

22- or 24-gauge wire for butterfly woman

Iron-on adhesive

CREATING THE UNDERSTRUCTURE

2. Following the procedures in step 1, cut and sew the understructure fabric for the torso, arms, and legs. Stuff the torso very firmly through the neck opening.

3. Cut a small hole at each shoulder for the arm wire. Cut a piece of 16-gauge wire long enough to go from one wrist through the shoulders to the other wrist. Push the wire through the shoulder openings. Thread the upper arm pieces and the lower arm pieces onto each side of the wire.

4. Firmly stuff the upper arm and lower arm. Slip-stitch the openings closed. Tack the lower arm to the upper arm at the elbow. Tack the upper arm to the torso at the shoulder. Your goal is to join the body parts without limiting the options for body positioning.

5. Cut two small holes at the bottom of the torso for the leg wires. Cut two pieces of 16-gauge wire that are long enough to go from the toe of the lower leg, through the upper leg, and through the torso to the neck. Twist the two wires together at the neck.

6. Slide the upper and lower legs onto the leg wires. Firmly stuff the pieces. Slip-stitch the openings closed. Tack the upper leg to the lower leg at the knee. Tack the upper leg to the lower torso. Bend the leg wires that exit the neck down into the torso. Close the neck opening so the neck wires disappear into the torso.

CREATING THE SKIN

7. Following the procedures in step 1, cut out and sew the skin-pattern pieces.

8. Lift the figure's arms, and pull on the torso skin. Sew the bottom of the torso skin closed. Pull the arm skin onto the arms. Pull the leg skin over the legs.

MAKING THE HANDS

9. Use figure 1 as a guide to shape the hand out of the 22-gauge wire. Use needle-nose pliers to pinch the wire fingers together. Wrap each finger and palm with transparent or floral tape. Splay the fingers far enough apart so scissors can cut between them.

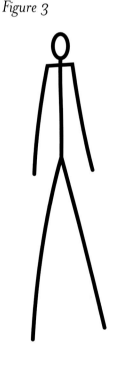

Figure 1

Hand

Figure 3

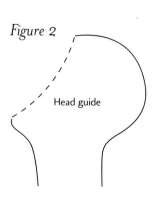

Figure 2

Head guide

10. Place the hands onto the cotton knit to make gloves. (Each glove's wrist opening must be big enough to accommodate the wire hand. You can squeeze the hand wire to make it fit.) With a light pencil, trace around the fingers to just below the wrist.

11. Sew on the line using a short stitch length. Trim to a $1/8$-inch (3 mm) seam, and turn right side out. Place the glove on the hand. Stuff the fingers lightly, and stuff the palm.

12. Push the lower arm and stuffing back from the arm wire. Use a smaller gauge wire to attach the hand wire to the arm wire. Secure the connection with hot glue. Pull the arm skin down to meet the wrist. Neatly stitch the arm skin to the hand skin, tucking any excess wrist fabric into the arm.

POSITIONING THE BODY & STUFFING UNDER THE SKIN

13. Pose the doll into the desired finished position. Note how the body reacts to this pose. It helps to put your own body (or a friend's) into this position, so you can see what happens as muscles contract, body fat folds, and skin hangs.

14. Use a stuffing tool or hemostat to stuff the arms with small pieces. Slide the stuffing into position with one hand, and hold it in place with the other hand. Release the stuffing tool and slide it out. Focus on the elbow and the upper arm muscles. Neatly stitch the upper arm skin to the torso.

15. Gently stuff the breast area and the abdomen if desired. Stuff and fill out the foot, ankle, calf muscles, knee, and thigh.

16. Stretch the excess leg skin up and over the lower torso. Place a large ball of stuffing at the top of the leg skin for the buttocks. Trim the excess skin to fit neatly between the legs at the bottom of the torso, and up and around each buttock. Sew the skin neatly in place.

COSTUMING THE DOLL

17. This figure's costume is made like a "crazy quilt." Cut a fabric circle with a 1-inch (2.5 cm) diameter. Use the glue stick to temporarily attach the circle to a starting point anywhere on the figure. Cut another 1-inch (2.5 cm) fabric circle. Glue the second circle next to the first with one edge slightly overlapping. Sew the pieces to each other and through the skin underneath.

18. Continue to add fabric circles until the whole body is covered. The costume evolves as it's being formed. You can accentuate body parts in many ways— by piecing the fabric into a corset at the breast and torso area; accentuating muscle contours; creating a spiral design that begins at the heart—the choice is yours. When attaching pieces, consider using embroidery thread and stitches. Embellish the figure with beads, stitching, or other design techniques. Stop costuming at the upper torso near the neck.

CREATING & ATTACHING THE HEAD

19. Using figure 2 as a reference, make an aluminum foil ball. Shape a neck cylinder from aluminum foil, and attach it to the head. Tilt the head into the desired position, relative to the body.

20. Wrap the head with plastic wrap, taping it at the neck. (The plastic wrap acts as a release agent.) Dip small pieces of torn paper into the glue or decoupage medium. Layer the paper strips onto the head like papier-mâché. Leave the head's opening free from paper. Make five or more paper layers; then let dry.

21. Slit the front of the neck, and gently lift the papier-mâché head off the aluminum foil. (If the head feels flimsy, layer more glue and paper.) Realign the neck slit and cover it with glue and paper. Let dry.

22. Hot glue the head and neck to the body. Costume the head and neck in the same manner as the body (see steps 17 and 18). Paint the inside of the head, or cover it with handmade or tissue paper.

CREATING THE BUTTERFLY WOMAN

23. Using figure 3 as a reference, create the basic figure from 22- or 24-gauge wire. Hot glue thin strips of aluminum foil around the body parts and head to add dimension. Apply thin strips of tissue or hand-made paper around the form with glue or decoupage medium. Let dry.

24. Cut out the photocopied wing patterns. Trace four upper and lower wings out of decorative fabric. Trace two upper and lower wings out of iron-on adhesive.

25. Make wing "sandwiches" with the adhesive layer in the middle of the fabric. Iron to bind the layers; then sew along the wing lines. Attach the upper and lower wings together in the center, then hot glue them to the butterfly woman. Hot glue the butterfly woman into the head opening.

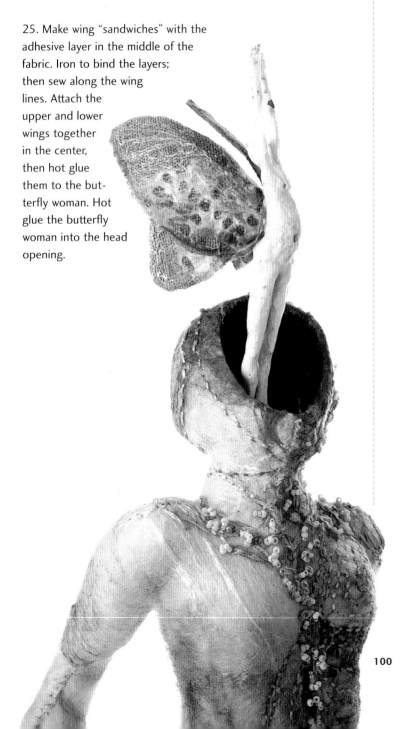

Margi Hennen
GREEN WOMAN

With all the energy of a wild garden, this doll is a champion of earthly delights. Luscious shades of green, multiple sprouting arms, and an overgrowth of hair symbolize organic vigor. Here's a great opportunity to cultivate your creativity.

FORMING THE BODY FABRIC ARC

1. Double the body fabric, right sides together. Lay the travel-size bottle on top of the body fabric. Draw an arc around the plastic bottle with a colored pencil.

2. Measure around the bottle's widest part. Extend the width of the arc drawn in step 1 so it's half this measurement, plus a little extra.

3. Measure the depth of the bottle at its deepest point. Make the arc longer than the bottle by this measurement. Add another $1/4$ inch (6 mm) to the length of the arc for the hem.

SEWING THE BODY FABRIC

4. Sew on the extended pencil line, leaving the bottom open. Trim the sewn fabric close to the seam line. Turn the fabric right side out, then push a little stuffing into the very top of the arc.

INSERTING THE TRAVEL BOTTLE

5. Place some sand or small gravel inside the bottle to add weight. Tuck the bottle into the sewn fabric arc. Turn the hem allowance under, making it even with the bottom of the bottle. Finger-press the hem in place.

MAKING & ATTACHING THE BASE

6. Stand the bottle upright on top of a piece of paper. Draw around the base of the bottle, holding the pencil as vertically as possible. Use this oval or circle to make a stronger template out of cardboard.

7. Glue the cardboard form to the wrong side of a piece of body fabric. Let the glue dry. Cut out the fabric surrounding the cardboard, leaving a $1/4$-inch (6 mm) hem allowance.

8. Glue the fabric-covered cardboard form to the bottom of the bottle. Use your needle to stick the extra fabric up under the hem as you slip-stitch it closed.

EMBELLISHING THE BODY

9. Apply surface treatments to the body fabric as desired. The designer applied delicate cross-stitch accents in assorted thin threads after she painted the body fabric in coordinating colors. You also could use stamping, drawing, or beading techniques.

CREATING & ATTACHING THE ARMS

10. Cut out two or more $3^3/4$ x $1^1/2$-inch (9.5 x 3.8 cm) pieces of green fabric. (You can vary the size of the rectangles for fatter or shorter arms.)

11. Fold the arm pieces lengthwise with their right sides together. Stitch one end and one side of each arm piece with a $1/4$-inch (6 mm) seam allowance. Trim the seam allowance close to the seam. Clip the corners of the sewn fabric. If you're using fabric that tends to fray, stabilize it with seam sealant. Turn the arms right side out.

12. Partially stuff the arms. Turn in and finger-press the hem allowance. Finish stuffing the arm.

13. Make small running stitches all around the open edge of the arm, and pull them up tightly. Take a couple of stitches across the gather to fasten your work; then take a backstitch, and push the needle back into the arm. Bring the needle out approximately 1 inch (2.5 cm) away. Clip the thread tail.

14. To form wrist and elbow joints, stitch back and forth through the arm in a single horizontal line.

15. Sew the arms onto the body.

CONSTRUCTING & ATTACHING THE LEGS
16. Draw two legs on a piece of paper, and cut them out. Trace around the legs on a piece of green fabric that is doubled, right sides together.

17. Stitch the fabric on the marked lines, leaving the top of the legs open for turning. Cut out the stitched fabric.

18. Partially turn the leg right side out. (It's easier to stuff the foot end if the leg is only slightly turned.) Stuff the leg partially, and then turn the top of the leg up all the way. Turn in the hem allowance. Stuff the rest of the leg.

19. Using two pins for each leg, position the legs on the body. Attach the legs by sewing around the thigh openings.

ADDING THE BREASTS
20. Using a beading needle, sew from the body through the large bead, through the seed bead, back through the large bead, and then into the body several times. (The seed beads hold the larger beads in place.)

MAKING THE FACE
21. Cut an oval piece of paper, and hold it on the doll to see if it's the right size for the face. Adjust the oval as needed.

22. Place the face pattern on top of the beige fabric. Trace the face pattern onto the fabric with a pencil.

23. Draw the facial features with the fine-point indelible pen. Color them with colored pencils. (Don't worry if you don't like your first face. Because you'll be appliqueing the face onto the doll, you can make as many faces as needed until you're satisfied with the drawing.)

24. Cut around the face about $1/8$ inch (3 mm) outside the pencil line. You can use pinking shears if you like. Fold-in and finger-press the seam allowance, or cut the seam allowance off if you prefer a frayed edge. Baste the seam allowance down.

25. Slip-stitch the face onto the doll's body, or use a different stitch to achieve unique effects. Remove the basting stitches.

EMBELLISHING THE DOLL
26. Bunch the chenille yarn, and sew it to the top of the head.

27. Cut small leaf shapes out of the body fabric, and sew them into the hair and around the face.

28. Sew miniature plastic vegetables, flowers, fish, tools, or whatever you wish to the doll's hands, arms, hair—anywhere!

Kathryn Belzer
BLESSING DOLL

Instead of rice to throw, lucky wedding guests often receive tiny bottles of bubbles to blow at the happy couple. This angelic blessing doll, crafted from a bubble bottle, was inspired by the promise and emotion of that special day. You'll enjoy weaving many eclectic elements into a cohesive and thematic design.

what you need

Basic sewing kit

Individual bubble bottle with dove cap (empty)

Multi-purpose glue

Small strip of thick white felt, or light-colored

Acrylic paints

Acrylic matte medium

Face from a magazine or catalog*

Cotton cloth for face, twice the size of bubble hoop

Darning needle

Tweezers

Telephone wire

Driftwood, with lichen if possible

Pebbles, sand, or aquarium gravel

Decorative threads

Large seashell for puff sleeve

Hand charm

Freezer paper

Cotton cloth for wing

Glue stick

Several small seashells

Small hank of dyed lamb's fleece

*This found image may inspire your whole piece, or you may have to search for a face that resonates with your idea for the doll.

PREPARING THE BUBBLE BOTTLE WAND & CAP

1. Remove the wand from the bubble bottle, and detach the wand from its cap. Keep the wand, as it will become the base for the face and neck.

2. Glue a thin strip of felt around the bottle cap. (This gives you a nice surface for stitching or gluing decorative accents later.) If desired, give the felt a wash of color with diluted acrylic paint. Set the cap aside to dry and bond.

"LIFTING" THE FACE

3. Apply thin coats of acrylic matte medium to the printed face. Spread the medium with a foam brush or credit card. Wash the spreader, and let the matte medium dry between coats. After three or four coats, leave it to dry overnight.

4. Soak the face in cool water, and gently rub off the paper. Trim your "lifted" face to remove any extra ink.

TRANSFERRING THE FACE TO CLOTH

5. Coat the cotton fabric for the face with matte medium. Gently press the "lifted" face onto the coated cloth. Let dry.

ATTACHING THE FACE, DRIFTWOOD & CAP

6. Cover the loop end of the bubble wand with the cloth face, and stitch it in place. The wand stem points down to become the neck. Paint additional facial details, such as eye color, over the matte medium if desired.

7. Use the darning needle to make two holes halfway up the opposite sides of the bottle cap. Feed the ends of the wire through the holes in the cap, grasp the ends with a tweezer, and pull them through. Adjust the wire so there is an equal amount on each side of the cap.

8. Position the driftwood behind the face, then set the bottle cap on top of both pieces. Cross the wire behind the driftwood and the face loop, and wrap the driftwood and the stem of the bubble wand together, leaving about 12 inches (30.5 cm) of loose wire on each end.

SETTING THE SHOULDERS

9. Weight the bubble bottle with pebbles, sand, or aquarium gravel. Make a hole on both sides of the bubble bottle at "shoulder" height. On the wing side, poke an additional hole below the first. Thread wires through the holes on the wing side, and wrap them with decorative threads. On the hand side, double the wire back over itself. Thread the large puff-sleeve shell over the wire. Wrap the wire and attach the hand charm with decorative thread.

CREATING THE WING

10. Draw a wing on the dull side of the freezer paper. Cut out the pattern and press it to the wrong side of the folded wing cloth. (You can press your pattern onto cloth another time or two, if you want to make more wings.)

11. Stitch around the wing, leaving the center back open for turning. Peel the freezer paper off the cloth. Trim away excess fabric; then turn and lightly stuff the wing. (Make a tiny wad of stuffing, and apply a little glue-stick glue before filling the tips of the wing. This keeps the stuffing from backing out of such extremities once they are blocked.)

12. Tuck one seam allowance inside the wing. Leave the other seam allowance untucked. Draw feather lines on the wing fabric with colored pencils, and then quilt along the lines with decorative thread. Glue the untucked seam allowance to the back of the bottle.

ADDING THE FINAL TOUCHES

13. Glue or stitch the tuft of fleece on top of the bottle cap. Tie a variety of decorative threads to the base of the dove. Ravel, twist, or otherwise modify the ends of the threads. Tie tiny shells to the ends of a few.

Kathryn Belzer. *Blessing Doll* (alternate design), 2001. Mixed Media. Photo by Keith Wright

DOLLS
for
Fertility

Today, in "civilized" societies, an eager couple might consult medical specialists to get help in conceiving, but since prehistoric times, people have turned to fertility figures, or Venus figures. With mammoth breasts and massive buttocks, these carved stone forms represent the fruitful Earth Mother.

The fertility of humans is vitally important to societies whose survival relies on large families. Africa is especially well-known for its fertility dolls. Varying greatly in size, some are carved from wood, and others are beaded. They sometimes wear jewelry, and all are female.

In some African tribes, small girls traditionally carried a spirit doll with them in preparation for marriage and childbirth. Imbued with a special magic, the doll had to be protected and cherished in order to fulfill its purpose.

The Bidjogo women of Guinea carve fertility dolls from forked-tree branches. They carry the dolls on their hips like a small child. The dolls have spread legs and no arms, with simple heads studded with nails or carved.

In the Ashanti tribe of Ghana, recently married women, or those wanting to conceive, carry a doll and treat it like a real child—nursing, bathing, dressing, and putting it to bed. (Some tribes in South Africa even name their dolls.) If a woman wants a beautiful child, she keeps a special doll in her waist cloths. If the mother-to-be desires a baby boy, she carries a doll with a flat moon-shape face. A small-headed doll is carried to create a girl. Ashanti women continue to wear the doll throughout their pregnancies to ensure a healthy baby. After the birth of a daughter, the mother may give the doll to her child to play with and to teach her child care. Mfengu women of South Africa do this and fashion a new doll to carry until their next child's birth.

Zulu brides keep fertility dolls beside their headrests. Among the Ewe of Southeastern Togo, the women keep dolls with broken arms or legs under their mattresses to ensure fertility. They consider dolls with broken appendages more powerful, a safeguard that children will be born healthy, with arms and legs intact.

If an African fertility doll fails to work, its owner may throw it away, give it to a child as a toy, or even sell it to someone who might have more success. If she suddenly conceives, she will consider the doll valuable and use it again.

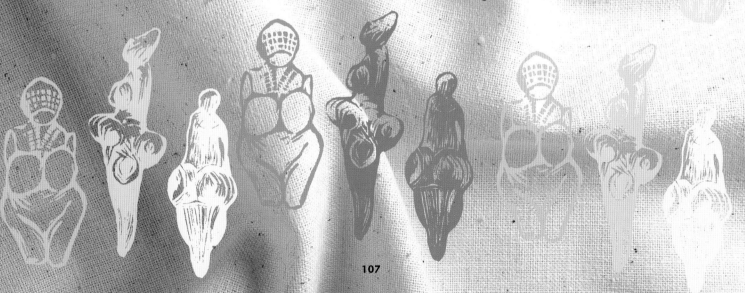

Lois Simbach
HEART'S DESIRE WISH DOLL

The Heart's Desire Wish Doll is a collage of individually selected images based around a specific theme. Depending upon your artistic eye and choice of materials, these dolls can express a single subtle yearning or many wild desires. Making this doll provides a great opportunity to focus on your lifetime goals, or celebrate the hopes of family or friends.

PREPARING THE PATTERN PIECES

1. Use a photocopy of the pattern provided, or design your own doll shape on a large piece of paper. Make the arms longer or the legs fatter—whatever suits your fancy. (You can fold the paper in half if you want to get both sides even.) Cut out the pattern.

2. Double the fabric, right sides together. Trace the pattern onto the fabric. Pin the fabric together on the marked line.

MAKING THE DOLL BODY

3. Sew within the tracing, leaving an opening at the top of the head. Cut out the figure with a 1/4-inch (6 mm) seam allowance. Clip all curves, and then turn the fabric right side out. Stuff the figure.

CREATING THE HAIR

4. Inside the wig, you'll see concentric circles of loosely attached ribbons of wig fibers. These can be cut apart easily to expose the long ribbon of wig hair. (Simply cutting hair from a wig won't work for this project. Because the hairs aren't bound, they'll easily fall out or be pulled out of the seam.) Hand-sew the ribbon of wig hair (or fringe or yarn) into the top seam of the doll as you close the head.

COLLECTING THE ORNAMENTS

5. Think about the focus of your heart's desire doll. What imagery do you want to apply? What words? Think of personal wishes, specific goals, and answers to life's questions. Where do I want to live? Who is my ideal partner and friend? What material do I want to own? What career do I want to pursue? Where would I like to travel? What character traits do I want to grow into? Find images and items to put on the doll that reflect one or as many of these queries as you like. You already may have a collection of tiny gizmos with special meaning, or you may have to keep your eyes peeled as you go about your daily life.

6. Laminate any paper item you intend to sew to the doll. Leave enough space around the word or image to make one or more holes in the plastic. The holes allow the item to be sewn to the doll. You also can laminate such items as dried flowers and butterfly wings.

CREATING THE FACE

7. The face could be a laminated photo of yourself, the person for whom you're making the doll, or even the person you desire. If you like to paint, the face could be created on muslin, and then appliqued onto the head. Or, as on the doll in the photo, the facial features could be an assemblage of found items, such as button eyes, an old buckle for a nose, and even a plastic lizard mouth!

EMBELLISHING THE DOLL

8. Use a beading needle when embellishing your doll as you'll want to frequently fill spaces and add color with seed beads. Sew through the items several times with doubled extra-strong hand-quilting thread. (These dolls often receive extra handling, so their decorations must be securely attached.) How fully you decorate the doll is up to you and usually depends on the amount of embellishments you collect to fit your theme. You can always add more elements to your personal doll.

9. Attach a small ring or a large eye (from a hook-and-eye set) to the back of the doll for hanging.

Arlinka Blair
KUBA SPIRIT

Exaggerated animal characteristics make Kuba Spirit a mysterious creature. African textile designs and bold linear embroidery contribute to the doll's dynamic essence. The tube–based form is simple to sew, and you'll have the opportunity to experiment with photocopy transfer techniques.

TRANSFERRING THE TEXTILE DESIGN

1. Take your Kuba cloth or photographic reproduction to a print shop, and have two color photocopies made on specially-coated transfer paper. Once home, set your iron on a high setting, and heat-transfer the photocopies onto the white cotton fabric.

PREPARING THE CLOTH

2. Cut out the photocopied pattern pieces. Double the fabrics with the right sides together. Trace the pattern pieces onto the appropriate fabric (see materials list) with a pencil or erasable marking pen. Cut out the pattern pieces, leaving a 1/4-inch (6 mm) seam allowance.

CREATING THE FACE

3. If you wish, add a thin coat of fabric paint or printing ink to the front side of the head, and let dry. (On this doll, the artist used brown fabric ink and let the black fabric show through at the eyes and sides of the mouth.)

4. Sketch the facial features for your doll onto the head with a white pencil or sewing chalk. Make your own original design, or follow the face template provided on page 154.

5. Set your sewing machine to a zigzag stitch, and follow the lines marked in step 3.

what you need

Basic sewing kit

7 1/2 x 4 inches (19 x 10.2 cm) (minimum) of Kuba cloth* or photocopied reproduction of similar textile design

1/2 yard (45.7 cm) of good quality white cotton fabric for body

Photocopied doll patterns, pages 154–155

1/2 yard (45.7 cm) of printed fabric for arms and legs

1/4 yard (22.9 cm) of black cotton fabric for hands, feet, and head

Fabric paint or printing ink, optional

Paintbrush, optional

Photocopied face template, page 154

Embroidery thread in black, white, and neutrals that match your fabric

*The design on the doll body is taken from a piece of African Kuba cloth from the artist's personal textile collection. You can choose any design that appeals to you. Photographs of textiles from books and magazines easily can replace actual ethnic fabrics.

ASSEMBLING THE HEAD & BODY

6. Sew the top edge of the front body piece to the lower edge of the front head piece on the marked line. Sew the top edge of the rear body piece to the lower edge of the rear head piece on the marked line.

7. Pin or baste the joined head and body pieces together, right sides facing. Sew the pieces together on the marked lines, leaving an opening at the top of the head. Turn the fabric right side out and firmly stuff the head and body. Sew the top of the head closed.

MAKING THE ARMS

8. Double one piece of the arm fabric, right sides together. Following the marked line, sew up the length and across the top of the arm. Leave the bottom of the arm open for stuffing.

9. Turn the fabric right side out. Stuff the arm loosely at the very top so it swings well when attached. Firmly stuff the rest of the arm to within 1/2 inch (1.3 cm) of the bottom edge.

10. Repeat steps 8 and 9 to make the second arm.

MAKING THE HANDS

11. Place two hand pieces together, right sides facing. (Make sure you have the front and back pieces for the same hand.) Sew around the pieces on the marked line, leaving an opening at the top of the hand for stuffing.

12. Turn the fabric right side out. Firmly stuff the hand to within 1/2 inch (1.3 cm) of the bottom edge.

13. Repeat steps 11 and 12 to make the second hand.

111

CONNECTING THE HANDS, ARMS & BODY

14. Turn under and finger-press the open edge of one arm and its corresponding hand. Add stuffing if needed to fill out the fabric. Stitch the arm and hand together with black thread.

15. Sew the arm to the correct side of the body at the shoulder. (These stitches will later be covered by embroidery.)

16. Repeat steps 14 and 15 for the second arm and hand.

MAKING THE LEGS

17. Double one piece of the leg fabric, right sides facing. Following the marked line, sew up the length and across the top of the leg. Leave the bottom of the leg open for stuffing.

18. Turn the fabric right side out, and firmly stuff the leg to within $1/2$ inch (1.3 cm) of the bottom edge.

19. Repeat steps 17 and 18 to make the second leg.

MAKING THE FEET

20. Place two foot pieces together, right sides facing. (Make sure you have the front and back pieces for the same foot.) Sew around the pieces on the marked lines, leaving an opening at the top of the foot for stuffing.

21. Turn the fabric right side out. Firmly stuff the foot to within $1/2$ inch (1.3 cm) of the bottom edge.

22. Repeat steps 20 and 21 to make the second foot.

CONNECTING THE FEET, LEGS & BODY

23. Turn under and finger-press the open edge of one leg and its corresponding foot. Add stuffing if needed to fill out the fabric. Stitch the leg and foot together with black thread.

24. Sew the leg to the bottom edge of the body with a light neutral thread that matches the fabric pattern. Make sure to attach the leg to the correct side of the body.

25. Repeat steps 23 and 24 for the second leg and foot.

STYLING THE HAIR

26. Use a coordinating color of embroidery thread to make a single row of fringe across the top seam of the head. To make the fringe, insert the needle just below the seam on one side of the head and gently pull it through. Leave at least 2 inches (5 cm) of thread trailing the insertion. Loop the needle back over the seam and re-insert it near the original piercing. Tightly pull the thread through to the other side. Repeat across the seam line. Clip the fringe to the desired length.

EMBELLISHING THE FIGURE

27. Use a running stitch and embroidery thread to highlight the facial features. Work with various colors of floss, but stay within the palette used on the doll. (The artist used five different shades of thread to accentuate this doll's face.)

28. With decorative stitching, highlight specific areas up and down the arms and legs of the doll and on the front of its body.

29. Apply sharply contrasting accents of thin white thread to the black hands and feet with a loose and irregular running stitch.

30. Use heavy embroidery thread and a tight running stitch to outline the doll's form. Begin under one ear and stitch to under the arm. Repeat on the second side.

31. Using the same technique as step 30, make decorative stitches down both sides of both arms, changing colors and breaking the line often for added interest.

DOLLS
of the
Pueblo

The Pueblo of North America believe in the blessings of supernatural beings. The term kachina refers to three specific aspects of nature—rain, good crops, and health—that the Pueblo attribute to the supernatural. In kachina dances, the Pueblo petition these spirits and give presents of kachina dolls.

According to legend, actual kachinas visited the Pueblos, bringing blessings and gifts, and teaching them to hunt and make arts and crafts. However, the two groups had a terrible fight, after which the kachinas refused to return. They did, however, allow the Pueblos to wear masks and costumes in their likeness, representing the now-absent spiritual beings. If the costumed men acted properly like kachinas, the spirits would possess them. Assuming the character of the kachina, the dancer lost his personal identity and the rain would come.

Pueblo men prepare for their ceremonies in underground rooms, called *kivas*, where they carve the Kachina dolls. The Zuñi tribe of the Pueblo people create dolls usually from pinewood with separately carved, articulated arms. The Zuñi dolls are generally taller and thinner than the dolls made by the Hopi tribe of the Pueblo. The Hopi use a solid piece of dried root from a dead cottonwood tree. The Hopi attach horns, ears, bulging eyes, noses, and other details with pegs. Finally, they paint the dolls (often with stripes) and decorate them with feathers, leather, and yarn.

During the ceremonies, the men dance, sing, and distribute gifts, including kachina dolls, to the children. The dolls are not playthings, but the children may carry the dolls around. They're meant to teach the child about the gods and the Pueblo's religious beliefs. Hung up on the walls by the Hopi, kachina dolls serve as a constant reminder of the supernatural beings. (The Zuñi, by contrast, hide their dolls.)

Kachina dolls are now popular collectors' items. The Hopi make extra dolls specifically to sell, although they never use these commercial objects in their ceremonies.

Gallery of MYSTICS

Megan Noël. *Yeti Doll*, 8 x 7 x 2 inches (20.3 x 17.8 x 5 cm), 1999. Bead embroidery on synthetic suede; seed beads, glass beads, pearls, sequins, silver charms. Photo by Theresa Batty

VISION
"I have been creating beaded dolls for several years. It is my most personal form of art. I consider doll-creating to be a shamanistic process." Megan Noël

Roxanne Padgett. *The Keeper*, 20 x 10 x 3 inches (50.8 x 25.4 x 7.6 cm), 1999. Sculpted face mask, fabric body, pieced clothing, paper-box beads, sticks, natural materials. Photo by artist

VISION
"One of a series of 'Keeper Dolls.' A box is underneath the doll to keep things—secrets, dreams, ideas, and more." Roxanne Padgett

Roxanne Padgett. *Earth Pair,* 15 x 9 x 1 1/2 inches (38.1 x 22.9 x 3.8 cm), 1999. Fabric, sticks, beads, shell, porcupine quill. Photo by artist

VISION
"Exploring the human form in pairs, with the use of natural materials." Roxanne Padgett

Anne Mayer Hesse. *Serenity's Storyteller,* 30 x 16 x 8 inches (76.2 x 40.6 x 20.3 cm), 2000. Cloth over wire armature, hand-beaded face, wrapping and stitching; exotic yarns, beads. Photo by Jerry Anthony

VISION
"The combinations of contrasting elements makes 'doll' (figure) making so experimentally fun for me. I like the softness of fibers next to the hardness of beads and wire; the warmth next to the coolness." Anne Mayer Hesse

Gabe Cyr. *The Supernatural*,
23 x 20 x 2 inches (58.4 x 50.8 x 5 cm),
2000. Fiber body built and stuffed on
branch armature, gourd head with pit-fired,
sculpted porcelain half-mask, hand-dyed,
stamped, and painted body fabric; silk drape
gathered with worked copper, overdrape is
handwoven ikat, beadwork dangles with
gourd and bamboo. Photo by Martin Fox

Arlinka Blair. *Mything Persons*,
20 x 11 inches (50.8 x 27.9 cm), 1999.
Linoleum-block print, vintage wool, silk
braiding, fleece, antique buttons, hand-
spun wool yarn, cotton embroidery
thread, tie silk. Photo by Jonathan Blair

VISION
"Before making this doll I had been
looking at a lot of medical and art photographs of conjoined twins. I became
fascinated with body connections and
distortions." Arlinka Blair

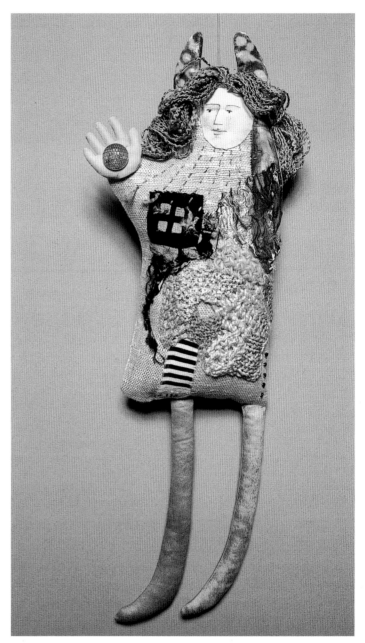

Arlinka Blair. *Santos,*
13 x 8 inches (34.3 x 20.3 cm), 2000.
Linoleum-block printing, decorative
machine-stitching, hand-quilting;
wishbone object, small Buddha pin,
wood, silk ribbon, thread. Photo by
Jonathan Blair

VISION
"This doll is from the series of religious
'Madonna' images. It is inspired from
the collection of Santos figures in
Mexican culture, particularly the
Guadalupe Madonna." Arlinka Blair

Margi Hennen. *Watching Woman,*
19 x 7½ x 3 inches (48.3 x 19 x 7.6
cm), 2000. Raw silk, discharged velvet,
printed fabric, knit and crocheted yarn,
threads, buttons

VISION
"This doll evolved from an effort to use
the soft delicate colours which I usually
avoid. (I tend to be overt; I love the
bright sun-suffused colours one sees in
Guatemala or Mexico.) To make the
knit/crochet patch, I chose soft moon-
struck colours. I did decide that they
needed punching up, hence the small
bits of black-and-white stripes and the
black 'window' patch, but I'm delighted
that I did manage to keep her as subtle
as she is—a watching, rather than an
acting woman. Her horns were going to
be shoes, but she liked them better on
her head, which seemed to accord with
the moon goddess image, so I let her
have it her way (as if I had any
choice)." Margi Hennen

Elsabé Dixon. *Cat and the Hatman*, 25 x 20 x 15 inches (63.5 x 50.8 x 38.1 cm), 2001. Wire armature, fiber-wrapped and stitched, ceramic face attachment

Christy Puetz. *Girl as Sandwich*, 7¹/₂ x 7 x 2 inches (19 x 17.8 x 5 cm), 1999. Machine- and hand-sewn body, flat-stitch seed bead application; cotton cloth, seed beads

VISION
"The dynamics between humans and the places that we let our minds wander. Testing one's self for constant imperfections, then realizing imperfectness is a good thing." Christy Puetz

Margi Hennen. *Mother Warned Me about Fishnet Stockings,* 12 x 4 x 2 1/2 inches (30.5 x 10.2 x 6.4 cm), 2000. Indigo-dyed fabric, marbled fabric, heavy machine embroidery, transfer-printed fabric, buttons, decorative fish

VISION

"Here I was playing with free machine embroidery on a not-very-interesting piece of marbled fabric. From there I chose fabrics which went with the embroidered piece; the checked piece was a piece of white satiny polyester with gold dots on which I had ironed checked paper that the supermarket had used to wrap flowers. (These are transfer papers which have been used in the commercial printing of fabric; there is often colour still transferable left on them.) I can't tell you how I decided that the indigo legs needed embroidered stockings, or how the fish got there—you never can tell with fish!" Margi Hennen

Olga Dvigoubsky Cinnamon. *Keeping You Close to My Heart,* 10 x 4 x 1 1/2 inches (25.4 x 10.2 x 3.8 cm), 2000. Crocheted; waxed linen thread, glass beads, cotton fabric stuffing. Photo by Jeff Owen

VISION

"The top half of this body actually opens up—is a pouch of sorts—to keep a lovely memory in perhaps." Olga Dvigoubsky Cinnamon

Sara Austin. *The Journey*, dimensions variable, 2001. Mixed media installation; hand-printed fabric with transfer techniques, crochet, felting, wood, wire. Photo by Monty Jessup

VISION
"This series of figures began with a childhood memory—the last time I played dolls with my best friend. I thought about the different paths our lives have taken. We all embark on a personal journey, accompanied by dreams and fears, meeting helpers and guardians along the way. Mother/helpers come in many forms into my life." Sara Austin

detail

detail

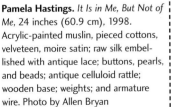

Pamela Hastings. *It Is in Me, But Not of Me*, 24 inches (60.9 cm), 1998. Acrylic-painted muslin, pieced cottons, velveteen, moire satin; raw silk embellished with antique lace; buttons, pearls, and beads; antique celluloid rattle; wooden base; weights; and armature wire. Photo by Allen Bryan

VISION

"I made a doll with a similar pose (inspired by a folk-art sculpture) for a show on healing and the arts. The rattle and reaching upward are meant to symbolize an affliction that may reside in one's body but does not represent the whole person. In other words, the person continues to be the person, above and beyond the illness. The rattle is pink on one side and white on the other. The handle of the rattle sticks out of the body on the left side of the doll, and the rattle can be rotated by the viewer (an engineering marvel), so either face can be toward the front. I'm not entirely happy with the proportions, but I was too far along to turn back, and sometimes misproportions can help to emphasize the feeling."
Pamela Hastings

Pamela Hastings. *Grandmother Box*, 14 x 6 x 4 inches (35.6 x 15.2 x 10.2 cm), 2000. Double buckram, antique picture frame, wire armature, quilt batting, felt, pieced cottons, batiked cotton, corduroy, synthetic suede, Thai silk, embroidery, photocopies, ribbons, feathers, decorative stitching, beads, multicolored embroidery thread with a metallic strand. Photo by Allen Bryan

VISION

"This is the first of the two architectural pieces, more poignant than overtly sad, as the other one turned out. I'll probably return to this theme again."
Pamela Hastings

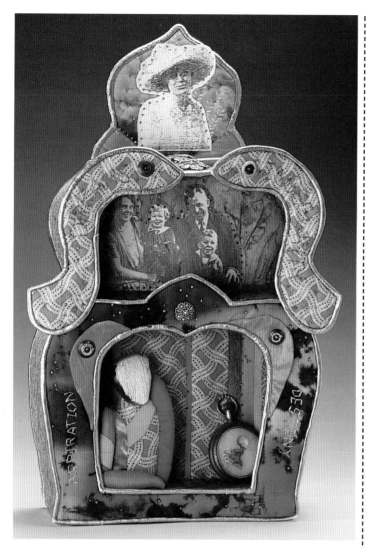

Pamela Hastings. *In My Grandmother's House*, 18 x 11 x 3 inches (45.7 x 27.9 x 7.6 cm), 2000. Double buckram, wood, quilt batting, felt, pieced cottons, corduroy, synthetic suede, Thai silk, lamé, antique buttons, watchcase, cotton, moth, beads, multicolored embroidery thread with a metallic strand. Photo by Allen Bryan

VISION

"The 'house' is built in the curvy shape of a woman, with a photocopy of my grandmother's high school graduation picture at the top as the head. Inside the 'chest cavity' is a photocopy of the only happy family picture I've seen with my grandmother: seated is her husband, and first two children—my mother and her older brother. There

was a great deal of tragedy in my grandmother's life, and I have done a number of works dealing with the family history.

The three-dimensional figure on the bottom 'floor' is an abstract representation of my grandmother's picture above. She ended up being strong and supporting herself and her children, although not always happily. The watch represents her father's business, the Leonard Watch Company, which supported them in style in her youth, but was totally lost during the Depression. Some of the embroidered words around the front are: aspirations, dreams, insecurity, destiny. 'It was not what I expected' is embroidered inside the top floor." Pamela Hastings

Sandy Webster. *Towanda/Lydia Series* (detail), 22 x 10 x 3 inches (55.9 x 25.4 x 7.6 cm), 2000–2001. Mixed media with found objects. Photo by Sandy Webster

VISION

"These reversible marionettes have been inspired by the impulses and extremes of two female myths: Fannie Flagg's controlled heroine Towanda of *Fried Green Tomatoes*, and John Prine's reclusive *Lydia*. Each bears the mark of her self-perception." Sandy Webster

Akira Blount. *Landscape Angel*, 24 x 7 x 5 inches (60.9 x 17.8 x 12.7 cm), 2001.
Cloth-over-cloth needle sculpture; fabric stiffeners, wood, acrylic paint, colored
pencil, leather, twigs (box elder), grapevine, pine needles, air-drying clay.
Photo by Tim Barnwell

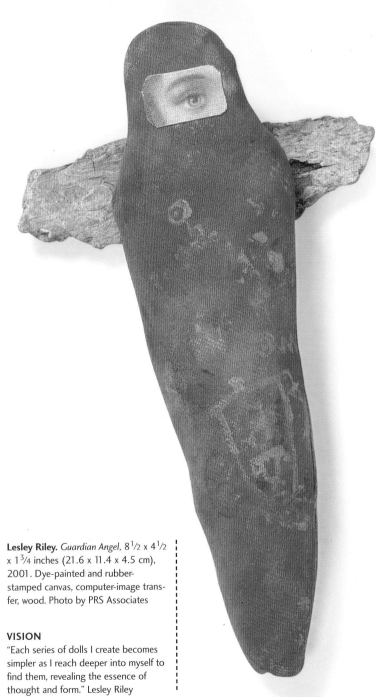

Lesley Riley. *Guardian Angel*, 8^1/$_2$ x 4^1/$_2$
x 1^3/$_4$ inches (21.6 x 11.4 x 4.5 cm),
2001. Dye-painted and rubber-
stamped canvas, computer-image transfer, wood. Photo by PRS Associates

VISION
"Each series of dolls I create becomes
simpler as I reach deeper into myself to
find them, revealing the essence of
thought and form." Lesley Riley

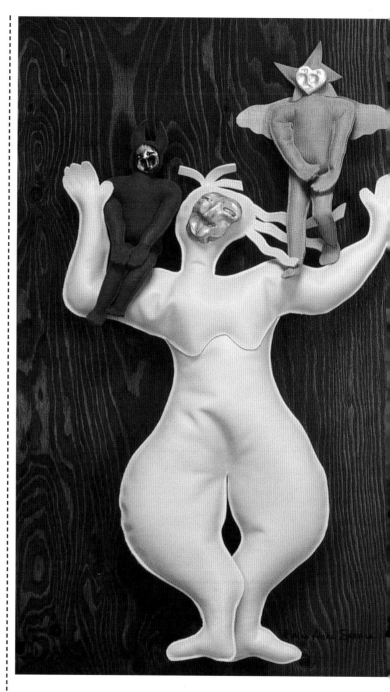

Anne Mayer Hesse. *Guardian Angel* (from the "Butterfly People" series), 60 x 28 x 14 inches (152.4 x 71.1 x 35.6 cm), 1999. Cloth over wood and wire armature, wings made by stitching yarns and beads onto old sweaters; exotic yarns, beads, monkey ladder vine. Photo by Jerry Anthony

VISION
"Some of the things that 'push my buttons' are: objects in nature; utilizing the 'what if' question; and colors, textures, and emotions." Anne Mayer Hesse

Elaine Anne Spence. *Good Enough Mom*, 33 1/2 x 25 1/2 inches (85.1 x 64.8 cm), 2001. Machine-stitched construction; commercially dyed leather, polymer clay, acrylic paint, metallic mesh, stained plywood. Photo by Bill Bachhuber

VISION
"Motherhood!" Elaine Anne Spence

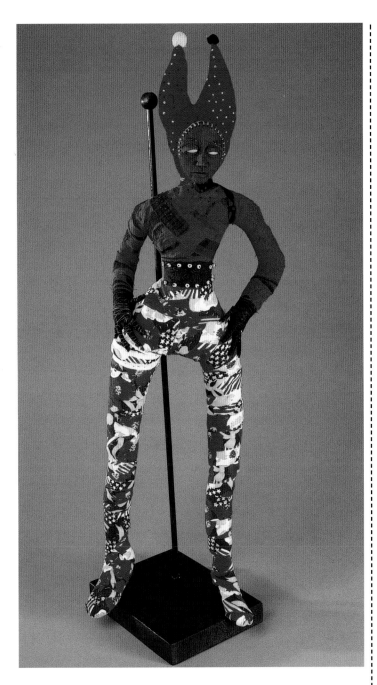

Elsabé Dixon. *Sassy Pants*, 23 x 10 x 7 inches (58.4 x 25.4 x 17.8 cm), 2001. Wire armature, fiber-wrapped and stitched, ceramic face and beads attached

VISION
"Inspired by the folk art of African mothers and religious and cultural icons, my work depicts fantasy figures that withhold stories." Elsabé Dixon

Christy Puetz. *Good Girl, Bad Things*, 19 x 9 x 6 inches (48.3 x 22.9 x 15.2 cm), 2000. Machine- and hand-sewn doll, various bead techniques, wood carving, embroidery; cotton cloth, seed beads, wood

VISION
"Any kind of indulgences can be okay in moderation; extremes (lots or none) can be unfulfilling and crazy. This doll is not about blame or regret, but about checking one's own limits, and also accepting them." Christy Puetz

Pattie Bibb. *Lepidoptera Dreams*, 17 x 20 x 12 inches (43.2 x 50.8 x 30.5 cm), 2001. Wire armature, batting, cloth, paperclay. Photo by Jerry Anthony Photography

VISION
"Paperclay over cloth combines my two favorite materials. Using this method, I have been able to produce the work as I see it." Pattie Bibb

Pattie Bibb. *Arachne*, 18 x 10 x 10 inches (45.7 x 25.4 x 25.4 cm), 2001. Wire armature, batting, cloth, paperclay. Photo by Jerry Anthony Photography

Olga Dvigoubsky Cinnamon.
Vassalisa's Doll, 12 x 6 x 1 ½ inches
(30.5 x 15.2 x 3.8 cm), 2001.
Crocheted; waxed linen thread, glass
and vintage beads, freshwater pearls,
cotton fabric stuffing. Photo by
Jeff Owen

VISION
Vassalisa's Doll is "from the fairy tale
Vassalisa the Wise. It was created for
the Once Upon a Time exhibition at the
Wustum Museum." Olga Dvigoubsky
Cinnamon

Kathryn Belzer. *Lady Godiva on Her
Way to a Tête-à-Tête with Laura Secord*,
14 x 16 x 14 inches (35.6 x 40.6 x
35.6 cm), 1999. Needle-modeled cotton sock, papier-mâché cloud. Photo by
Dan Abriel

VISION
"Lady Godiva was a courageous activist
whose name is now associated with
chocolates." Kathryn Belzer

Kathryn Belzer. *Laura Secord waits to share confections and discuss activism with Lady Godiva,* 13 x 16 x 15 inches (33 x 40.6 x 38.1 cm), 1999. Needle-modeled cotton sock body, silk clothing and wings, papier-mâché cloud, polymer clay candies. Photo by Dan Abriel

VISION

"Laura Secord was a Canadian hero of the War of 1812. She ran through miles of difficult swampland to warn the British of a planned attack from the south. Today, Laura Secord Chocolate Shops are very popular in Canada."
Kathryn Belzer

detail

Gabe Cyr. *Budd-ha,* 23 x 12 x 9 inches (58.4 x 30.5 x 22.9 cm), 2000. Carved, engraved, dyed, hinged, and waxed gourd; fiber, sculpted and metal-licized polymer clay, beaded, embroidered. Photo by Martin Fox

VISION

"The media I've explored over the past 30 years as an artist all find their way into my figure work—and half of the found objects I've tripped across too!"
Gabe Cyr

Lois Simbach. *Flora and Fauna Flower Doll*, 14 inches (35.6 cm), 1998. Mixed-media fabric construction featuring laminated butterfly wings

VISION

"Created for a group exhibit based on theme of Monet's garden." Lois Simbach

Deborah C. Pope. *Haemish*, 23 x 11 x 12 inches (58.4 x 27.9 x 30.5 cm), 1999. Gotland wool with wire armature; hand-felted in the traditional hot-water-and-soap technique, sculpted before and after felting with felting needles. Photo by artist

VISION

"I never know what the final figure will be. The personality evolves. Haemish looked like the Michelin man until he shrunk in the felting process. He ended up resembling my husband without his mustache!" Deborah C. Pope

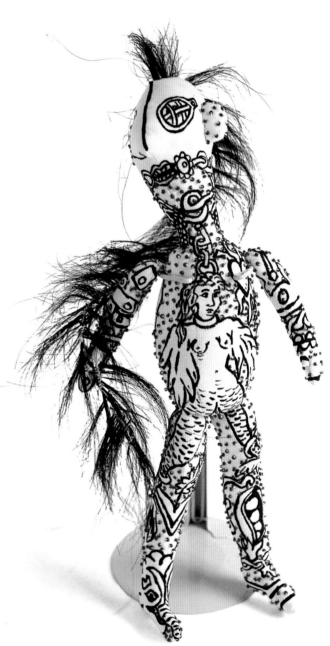

Akira Blount. *Dancers*, 31 x 19 x 9 inches (78.7 x 48.3 x 22.9 cm), 2001. Cloth-over-cloth needle sculpture; fabric stiffeners, wood, acrylic paint, colored pencil, leather, twigs (Tulip poplar), grapevine, pine needles, airdrying clay. Photo by Tim Barnwell

VISION

"My work is a combination of materials I love—cloth and natural materials. The figures depict personified images of the spirit of the woodlands." Akira Blount

Lois Simbach. *Albrecht Dürer Doll*, 12 inches (30.5 cm), 1999. Hand-painted fabric, seed beading, horsehair

VISION

"The hand-painted imagery was taken directly from Albrecht Dürer's etching *Maximillian's Triumphal Arch*." Lois Simbach

Patti Medaris Culea. *Jubilant Juliette*
(detail)

Patti Medaris Culea. *Jubilant Juliette*, 17 x 6 x 2 inches (43.2 x 15.2 x 5 cm), 2001. Dyed, painted, stamped, beaded, and needle-sculpted cotton and silk fabric with free-hand machine embroidery, mohair, and other decorative accents. Photo by Keith Wright

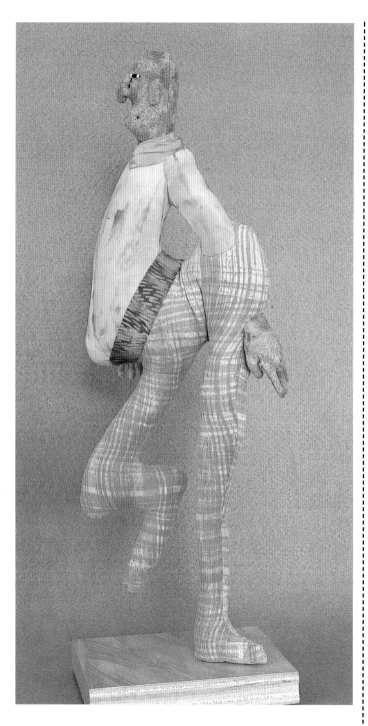

Deb Shattil. *Whistling Man,* 15 1/2 x 4 x 5 inches (39.4 x 10.2 x 12.7 cm), 2000. Wire armature, hand-painted fabric, wooden base. Photo by artist

VISION

"Sometimes I leave out body parts in favor of a nice silhouette. I describe the figure with shapes instead of anatomy." Deb Shattil

Deb Shattil. *Swaybacked Woman,* 19 3/4 x 4 1/2 x 5 inches (50.2 x 11.4 x 12.7 cm), 2001. Wire armature, fabric, beaded hair, needle-sculpted features. Photo by artist

Dee Dee Triplett. *Stretching Cat,* 14 x
5 x 2 inches (35.6 x 12.7 x 5 cm),
1998. Fabric, hand-forged iron base.
Photo by Evan Bracken

VISION
"Cats are stretch masters—one of my
goals is to cause you to feel the gesture
of the figure when you see my work."
Dee Dee Triplett

DOLL PATTERNS

Blank Canvas Projects, Clarity, page 32

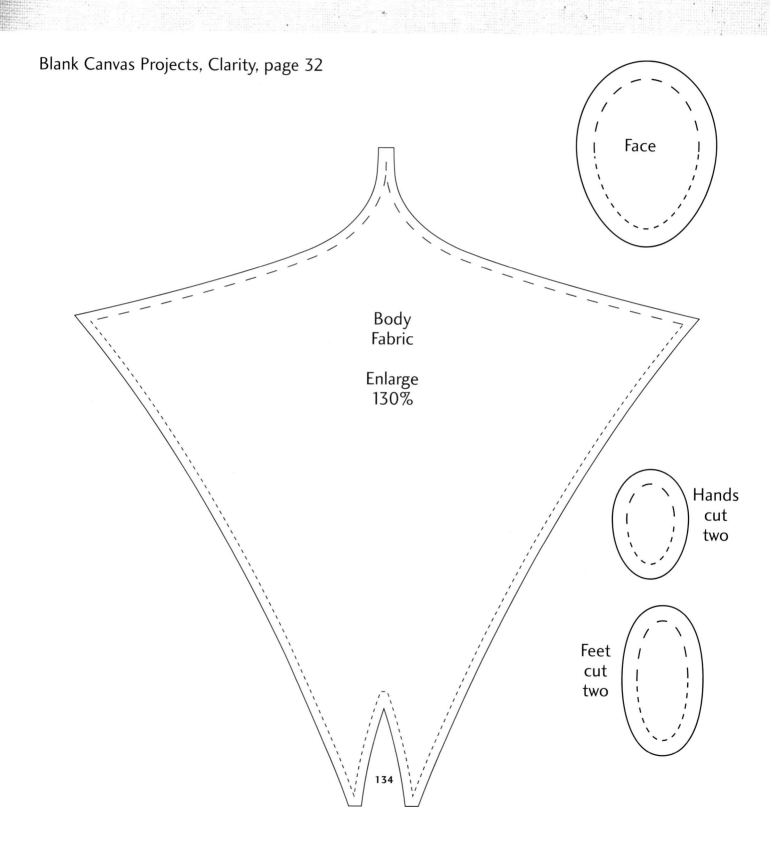

Face

Body
Fabric

Enlarge
130%

Hands
cut
two

Feet
cut
two

134

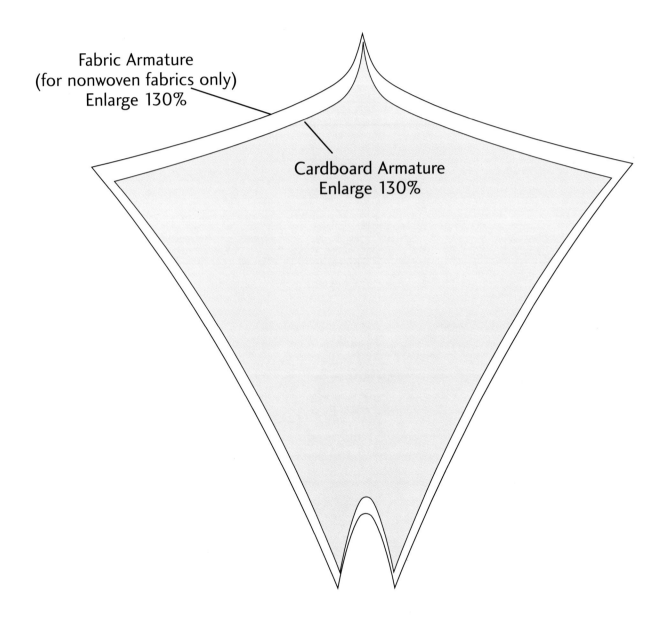

Fabric Armature
(for nonwoven fabrics only)
Enlarge 130%

Cardboard Armature
Enlarge 130%

Lynn Sward's Clarity, page 37

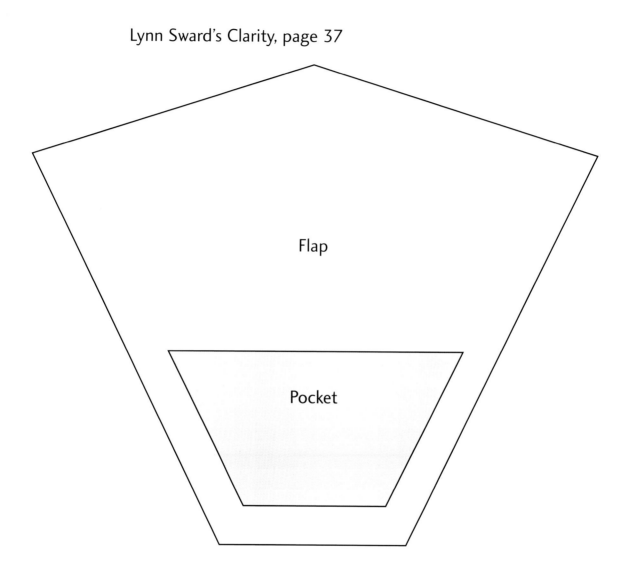

Flap

Pocket

Arlinka Blair's Clarity, page 39

Serpent Template for Linoleum Block

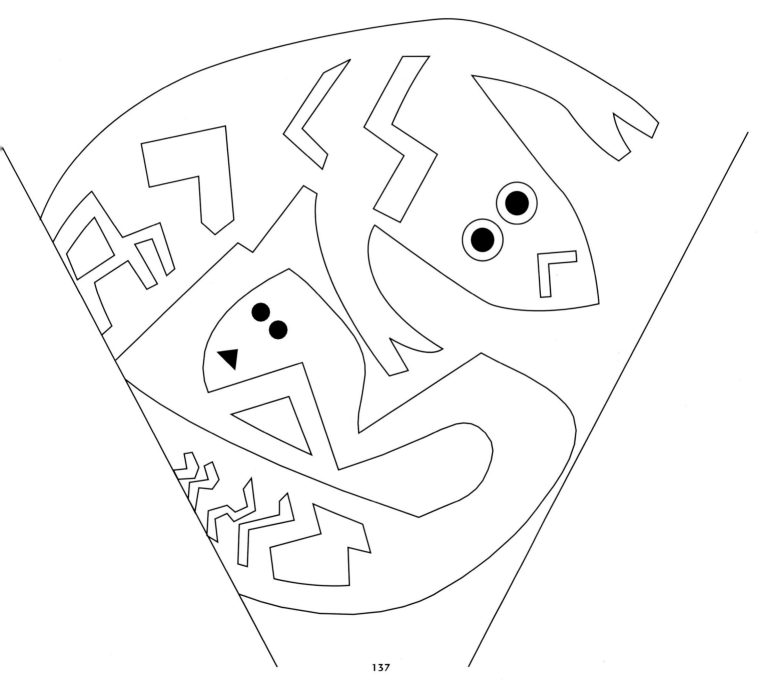

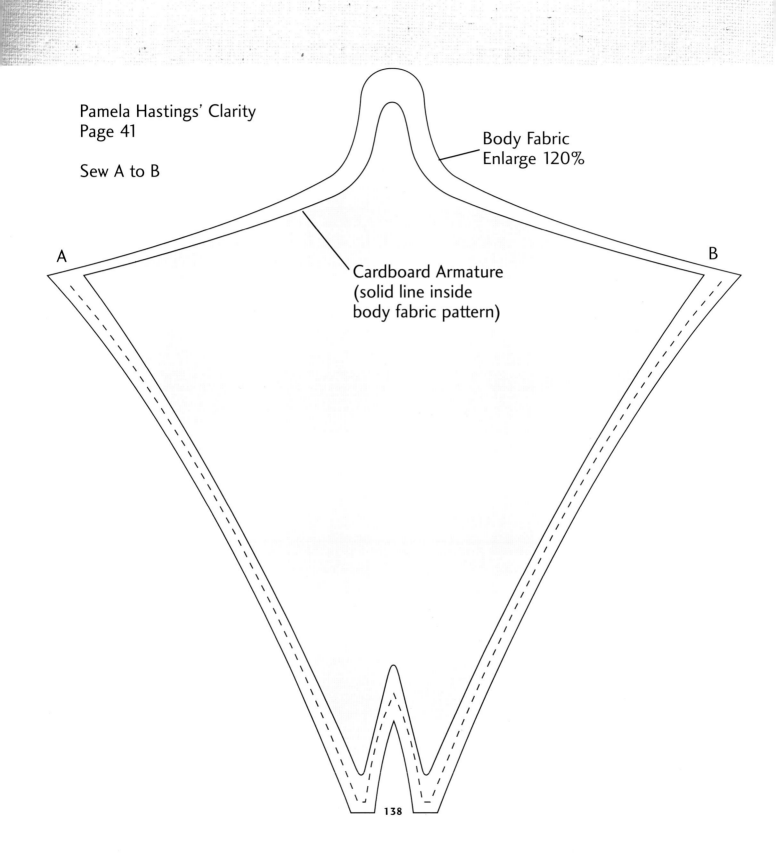

Pamela Hastings' Clarity
Page 41

Sew A to B

Body Fabric
Enlarge 120%

A

B

Cardboard Armature
(solid line inside
body fabric pattern)

138

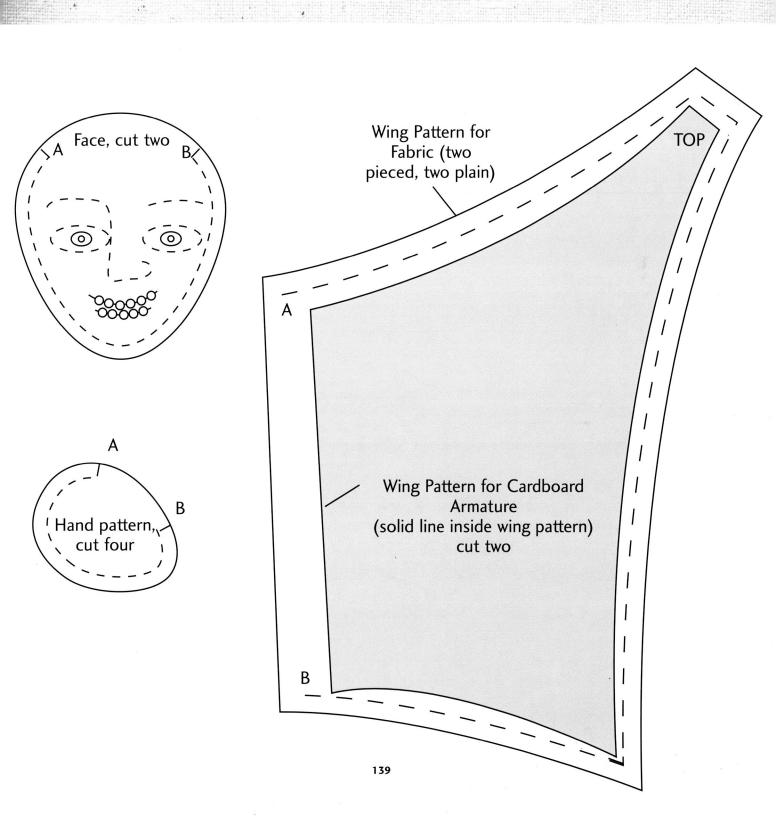

Face, cut two

A   B

A

B

Hand pattern,
cut four

Wing Pattern for
Fabric (two
pieced, two plain)

TOP

A

Wing Pattern for Cardboard
Armature
(solid line inside wing pattern)
cut two

B

139

Barbara Carleton Evans' Clarity, page 44

Applique Patterns, enlarge all 125%

Horse Ear, cut two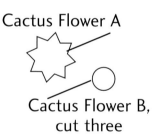

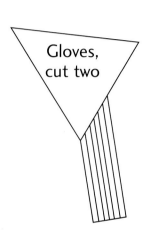
Gloves,
cut two

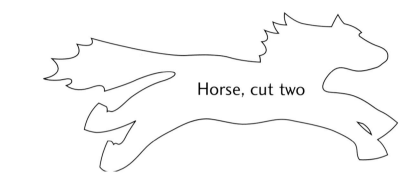
Horse, cut two

Boots

Hat
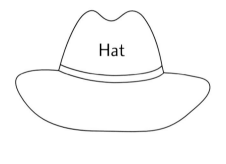

Cactus Flower A
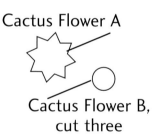
Cactus Flower B,
cut three

Sun, part
3 of 3

Sun,
part 2
of 3

Cactus A
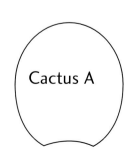

Sun, part
1 of 3
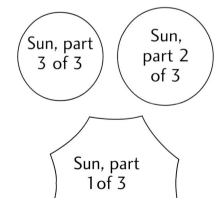

Cactus
B
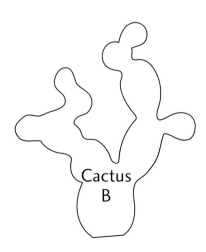

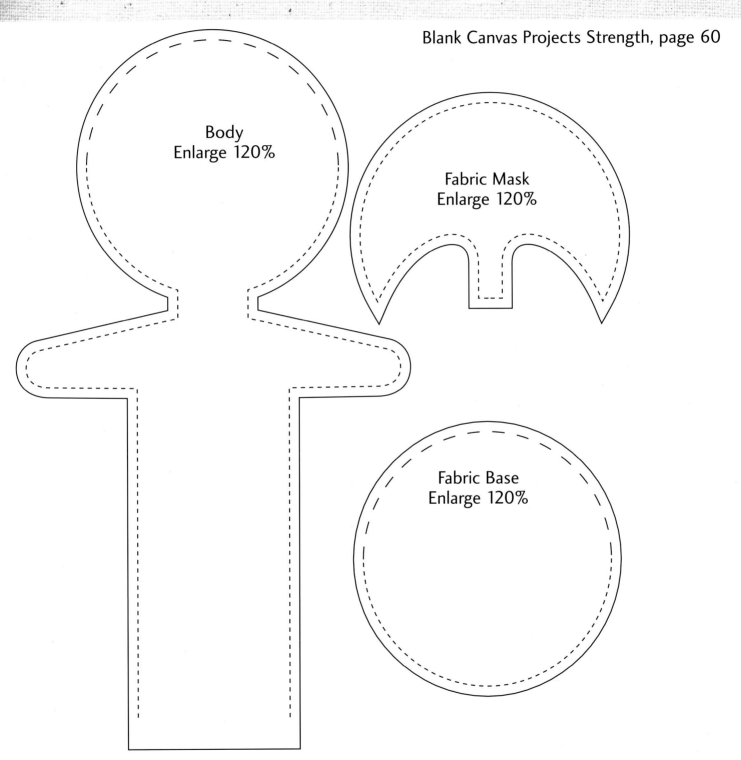

Body
Enlarge 120%

Fabric Mask
Enlarge 120%

Fabric Base
Enlarge 120%

Blank Canvas Projects Strengths
Page 60 (continued)

Cardboard
Armature for Mask
(woven cloth only)
Enlarge 120%

Cardboard Armature
for Base and Head

3-inch diameter (7.6 cm)

Cut two

Cardboard Armature
for Base
1-inch diameter
(2.5 cm)

Pamela Hastings'
Strength
Page 63

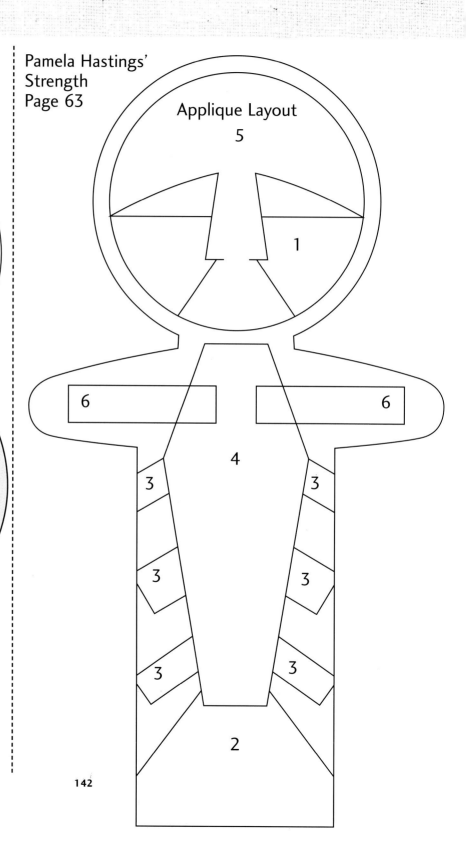

Applique Layout

5

1

6

6

4

3

3

3

3

3

3

2

Note:
Each Applique Piece 3 is a ½ x 1-inch (1.3 x 2.5 cm) rectangle
Each Applique Piece 6 is a ½ x 2-inch (1.3 x 5 cm) rectangle, Enlarge all 120%

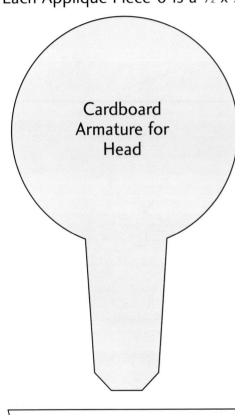

Cardboard Armature for Head

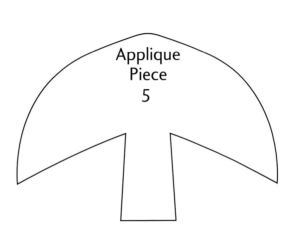

Applique Piece 5

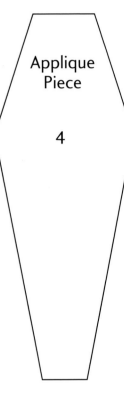

Applique Piece 4

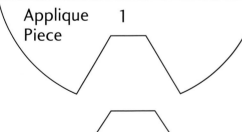

Applique Piece 1

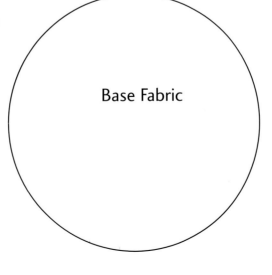

Base Fabric

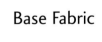

Base Fabric

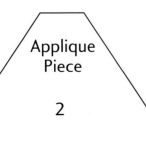

Applique Piece 2

143

Lynne Sward's Strength
Page 66

Face
Template

Barbara Carleton Evans'
Strength
Page 69

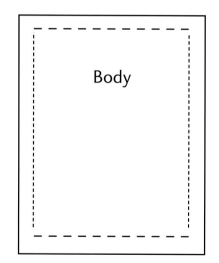

Breast,
cut two

Blank Canvas Projects, Energy, page 46
Enlarge 150%

Body

Lower
Arms

cut two

Upper
Arms

cut two

Legs

cut four

Head

Stick Guy, page 78

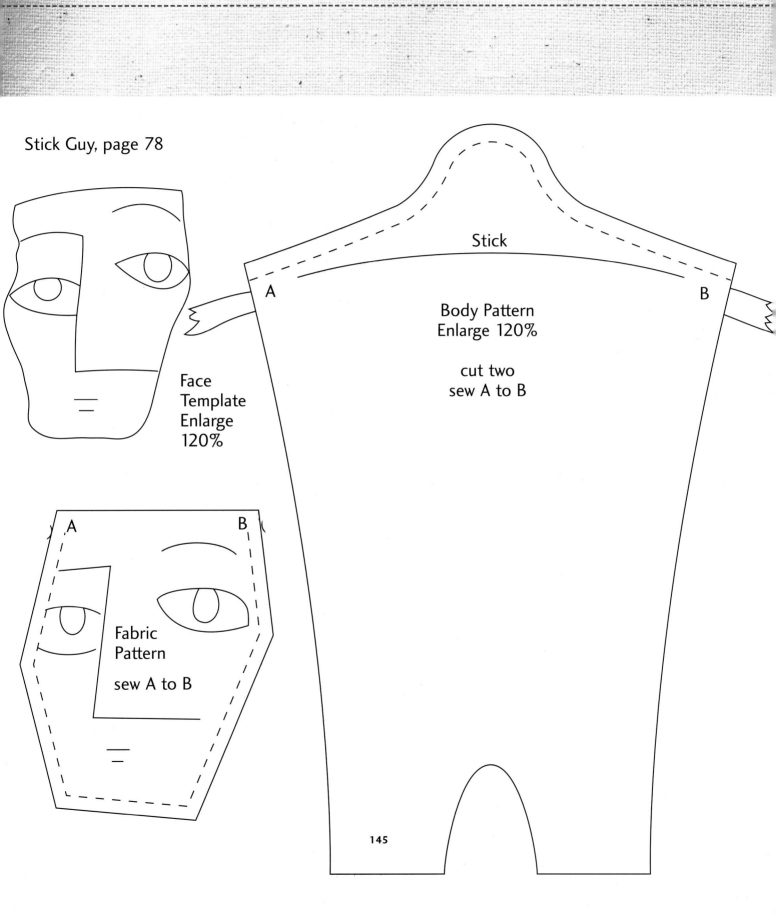

Face
Template
Enlarge
120%

A

B

Fabric
Pattern

sew A to B

Stick

Body Pattern
Enlarge 120%

cut two
sew A to B

A

B

145

Stick Guy
Page 78
(continued)

Enlarge all
Patterns
on this page
120%

Sew A to B

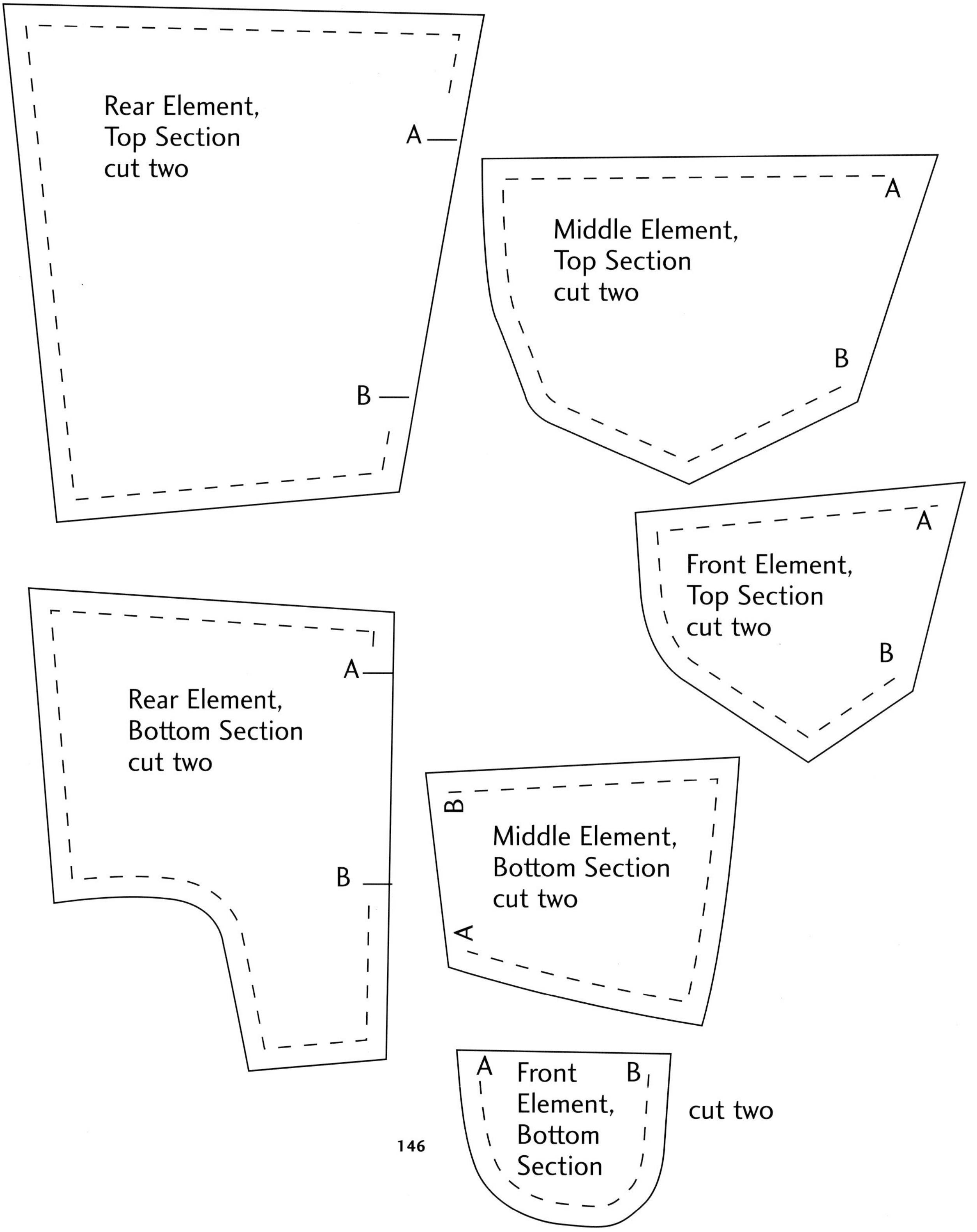

Rear Element,
Top Section
cut two

A —

B —

Middle Element,
Top Section
cut two

A

B

Rear Element,
Bottom Section
cut two

A —

B —

Front Element,
Top Section
cut two

A

B

B

Middle Element,
Bottom Section
cut two

A

A   Front   B
     Element,   cut two
     Bottom
     Section

146

Wily Woman
Page 81

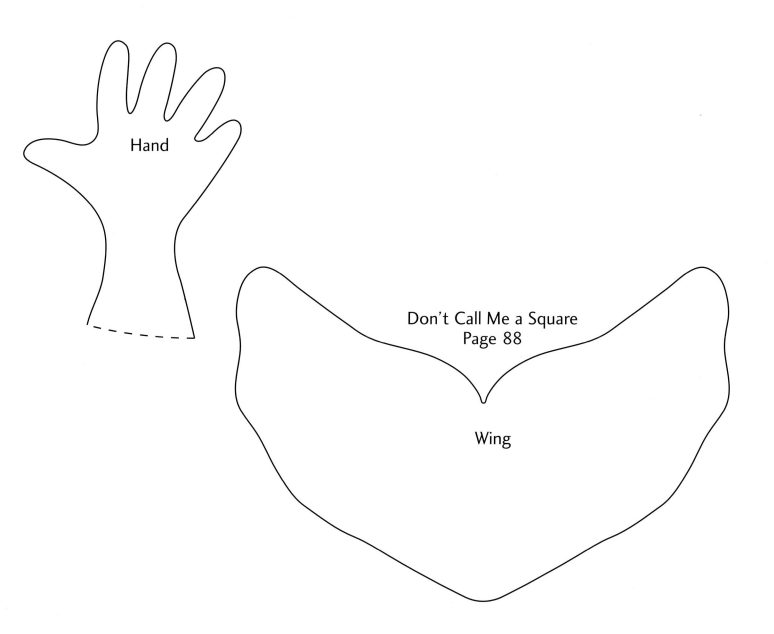

Hand

Don't Call Me a Square
Page 88

Wing

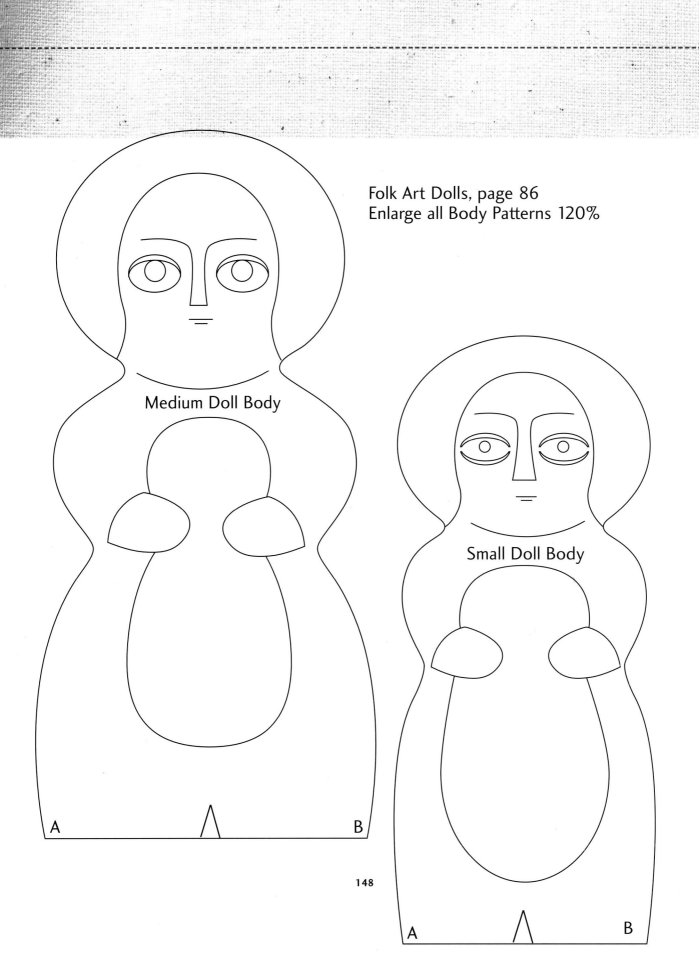

Folk Art Dolls, page 86
Enlarge all Body Patterns 120%

Medium Doll Body

Small Doll Body

A   B

A   B

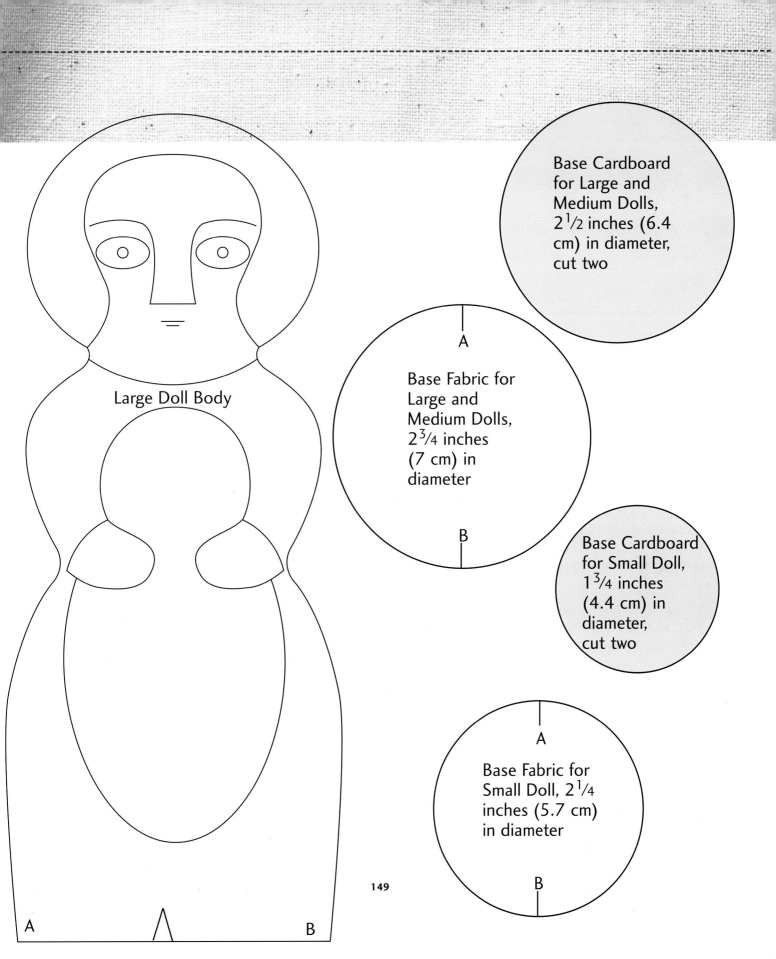

Large Doll Body

Base Cardboard for Large and Medium Dolls, 2$\frac{1}{2}$ inches (6.4 cm) in diameter, cut two

A

Base Fabric for Large and Medium Dolls, 2$\frac{3}{4}$ inches (7 cm) in diameter

B

Base Cardboard for Small Doll, 1$\frac{3}{4}$ inches (4.4 cm) in diameter, cut two

A

Base Fabric for Small Doll, 2$\frac{1}{4}$ inches (5.7 cm) in diameter

B

A   B

149

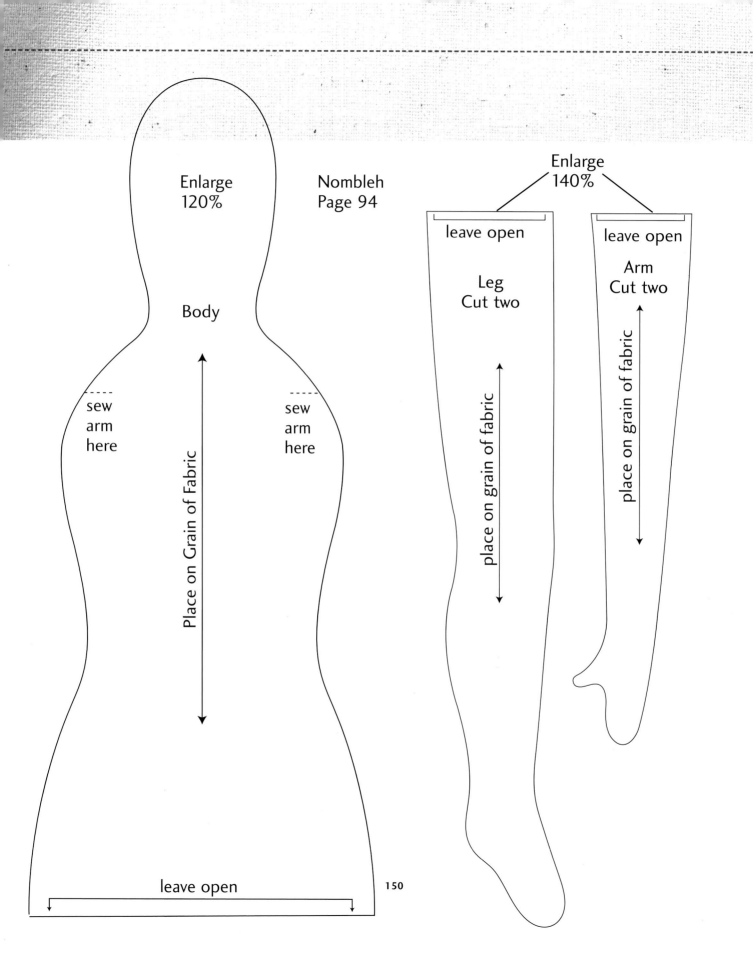

Enlarge
120%

Nombleh
Page 94

Body

sew
arm
here

sew
arm
here

Place on Grain of Fabric

leave open

Enlarge
140%

leave open

leave open

Leg
Cut two

Arm
Cut two

place on grain of fabric

place on grain of fabric

Metamorphosis
Page 97
Enlarge all 120%

Open

Torso Understructure

Cut two of muslin

Open

Upper Leg
Understructure

Cut four
of muslin

Upper Arm
Understructure
Cut four of
muslin

Open

Lower Arm
Under-
structure

Open

Open

Lower
Leg Understructure
Cut four of Muslin

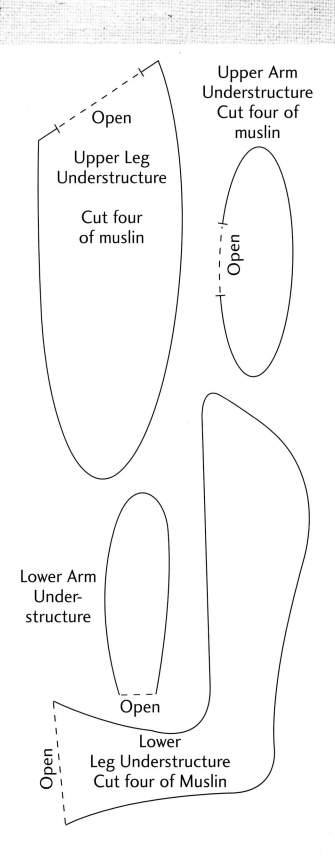

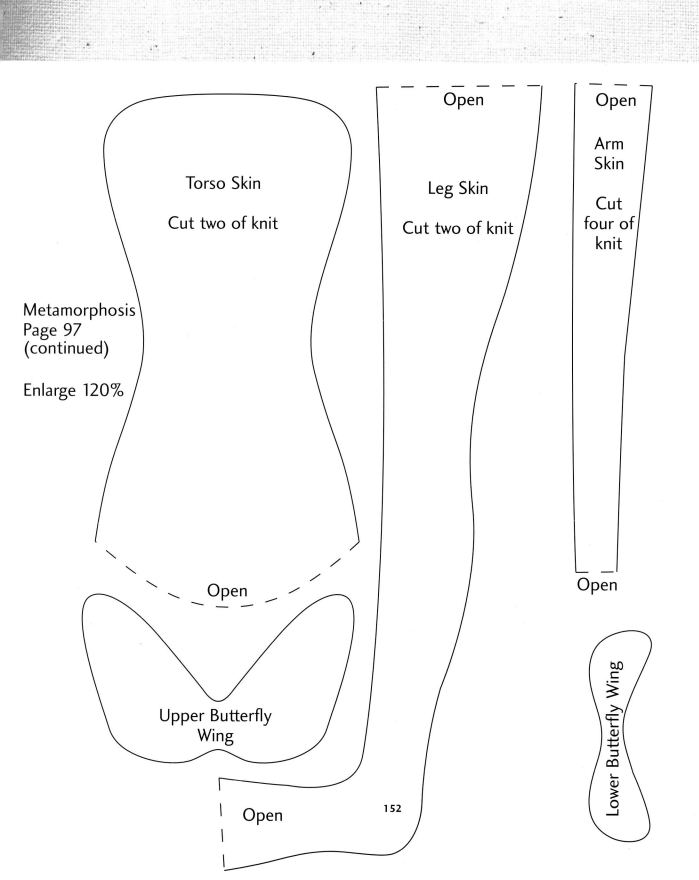

Torso Skin

Cut two of knit

Metamorphosis
Page 97
(continued)

Enlarge 120%

Open

Upper Butterfly
Wing

Open

Open

Leg Skin

Cut two of knit

Open

Open

Arm
Skin

Cut
four of
knit

Open

Lower Butterfly Wing

152

Heart's Desire Wish Doll
Page 108

Enlarge 165%

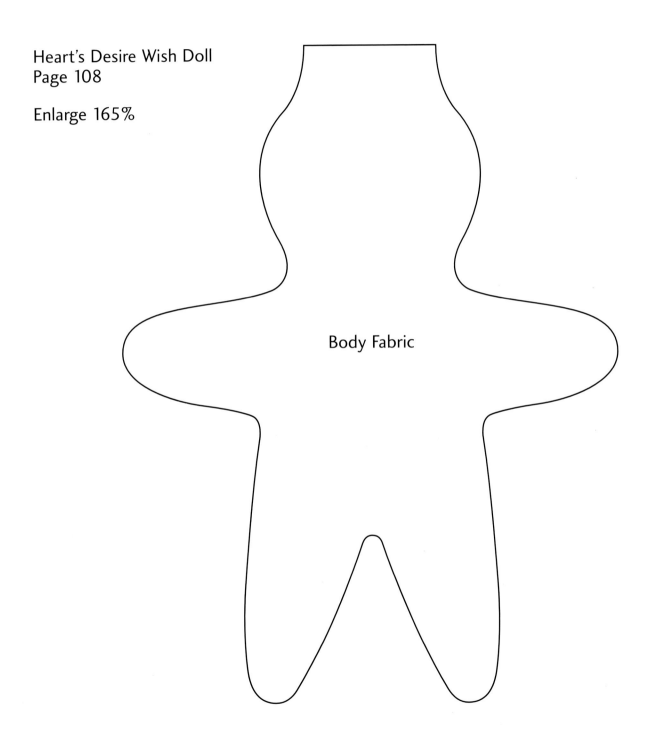

Body Fabric

Kuba Spirit ,Page 110
Enlarge 120%

Face Template

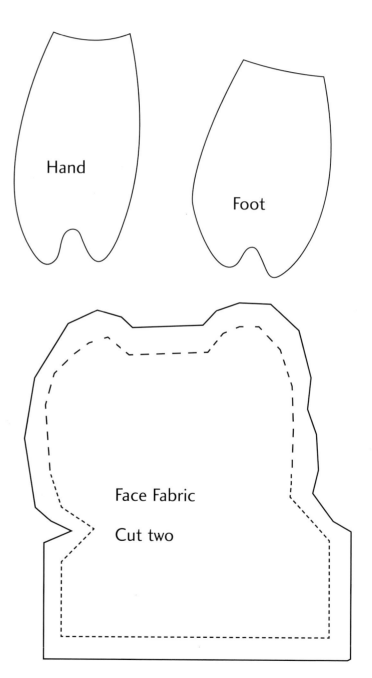

Hand

Foot

Face Fabric

Cut two

Body Fabric

Cut two

Enlarge 150%

Leg
Fabric

Cut
two

Enlarge
150%

Open

Arm
Fabric

Cut
two

Enlarge
150%

Open

CONTRIBUTING DESIGNERS

Kathryn Belzer lives with her husband, Ed, and a host of other creatures, on a small horse-powered farm in the Musquodoboit Valley of Nova Scotia. There is one house visible from one window of her farmhouse. Other than that, the "neighborhood is fairly quiet."

Kathryn has been a pattern-maker for theater, film, touring, and reenactment companies. Dollmaking has been a lifelong passion. Her empty nest and husband's retirement have fostered a greater concentration on studio work, dollmaking, and teaching. In the fall of 1998, Kathryn moved into a new detached studio space, and "hasn't stopped smiling since."

Arlinka Blair is at home in the spirit world. Motivated by a life-long interest in textiles, her work focuses on tribal and primitive cultures. She has traveled with the Hoxie Brothers Circus working as a clown, lived on the Mediterranean island of Cyprus where she became a scuba diver, and regularly joins the staff of the Hui Ho' olana Retreat Center on Molokai, Hawaii.

Arlinka began her career as an artist/teacher, graduating from the State University of New York at Buffalo. She also attended the University of Sienna, Italy, and the School for American Craftsmen at the Rochester Institute of Technology.

Later, as Arlinka traveled with her photographer husband, exposure to exotic cultures sharpened her vision. She was always on the lookout for unusual fabrics and village crafts. These bits and pieces would later start appearing on her quilts and dolls. Today Arlinka continues her travels within her art, working on ideas that celebrate inner journeys and the joy of creation. Visit Arlinka Blair's website at www.arlinka.com.

Beth Carter was a "closet creative" for more than 30 years. She jumped into the creative life after the births of her two children and the freeing of her long-latent artistic impulses. Her non-traditional art dolls are a blending of her love of textiles, words, tradition, and whimsy. Through her dolls she finds a means of expression that is like breathing, which often leaves her wondering how she survived all those years without them. Beth also gives lectures on finding personal creativity, and teaches workshops on non-traditional art dolls and mixed media assemblages.

Barbara Carleton Evans' childhood dolls were loved thoroughly, and frequently joined her for tea parties, walks on the beach, and explorations of the rhododendron-filled forest surrounding her home.

Barbara continued playing with dolls as an older child, making some from clothespins, flowers, and other found materials, as well as dressing her store-bought dolls. Barbara also made clothes for her daughter's dolls until horses became more interesting. Sewing horse blankets wasn't artistically challenging enough, so Barbara continued playing with dolls on her own. As her dollmaking skills improved, Barbara became frustrated by poorly-drafted commercial patterns, so she began to design her own patterns. Gradually, Barbara moved from using fabric to using hand-made felt, found objects, natural materials, beads, and anything else that had an interesting texture, shape, or color, as the components of her dolls.

Barbara's work found its way into craft magazines, doll magazines, and books.

Pamela Hastings has been sewing, drawing, and making dolls since she was five and couldn't start school with the rest of her friends. She has exhibited and taught nationally, and her work can be seen in many publications. Pamela's studio overlooks a pond in Saugerties, New York. Her interest in the process of creativity translates into her goal of giving her students the tools and jumping-off points to help them tap into their own creativity, as well as to create a finished product in her classes. Pamela's work "is a constantly evolving and vital aspect of a life spent drawing and creating. I am having a lifelong love affair with colors, images, fabrics, bits, and pieces. There is never an end to new combinations, new discoveries, new layers of meaning."

Margi Hennen is an art-school trained artist and a self-taught dollmaker (who never had the nerve to mention dolls at art school!)

Her dolls are a whimsical take on what it's like to be an aging, generously proportioned female in a world where the young and slender are the icons of the day. She is a wife, mother, grandmother, and content with all, given sufficient studio time.

Margi has taught and lectured in Canada, the United Kingdom, and Australia. Her work is represented in collections in North America, Europe, and Australia.

JoAnn Pinto has been teaching dollmaking nationally for 10 years. Her works have been displayed at fine galleries and shows including the New York Toy Fair and the Santa Fe "Doll as Art" show. Her dolls have been showcased on Home and Garden Television, the Carol Duvall Show, and in Contemporary Doll Collector magazine. She lives in Colorado with her husband and two sons.

Lois Simbach has a Bachelor of Science in textiles and fashion from the University of Wisconsin, Madison, and a Bachelor of Fine Arts in sculpture and art education from the University of Wisconsin in Milwaukee. Lois spent 10 years as a fashion designer in the garment industry and five years as a costume designer for theater, film, and television. She is the designer and owner of a doll and fashion wholesale and retail business. Products she has developed include "Ju-Ju of the Vieux Carre," a New Orleans voodoo-inspired embellished soft sculpture line. Lois has exhibited her dolls, sculpture, and paintings often, as well as been involved in performance art.

CONTRIBUTING DESIGNERS CONTINUED

Tracy Stilwell is emerging from traditional roots and has become a nationally known creator of quilts, non-traditional dolls, and wearables of many sorts. Her serendipitous artistic process brings a new level of expressive freedom to these old crafts. Tracy's art quilts are full of brilliant bursts of color and texture. Perceived as someone working on the edge, she often incorporates political and personal messages around the unpredictable combination of cloth, paint, wood, beads, bones, polymer and paperclay, rope, twigs, roots, yarns, threads, and found objects.

Tracy Stilwell knows how the inner critic can keep creativity at bay, so as a teacher in the doll world she encourages others to take risks, to be brave, and to defy the oppression of perfectionism. She encourages others to trust their own visions and uses of materials.

Practicing truth and gratitude, staying with the stitching, keeping the machine oiled, and snacking for strength, she continues down the path of a somewhat remarkable and very full life.

Lynne Sward has always loved making things. Art was her favorite subject throughout all her school years. On a summer trip in 1974 to her hometown of Chicago, a quilt show at the Chicago Art Institute forever changed Lynne's life. Those quilts demonstrated the color, craft, and design capabilities prevalent in other masterful media such as paintings, and she was totally hooked! Lynne decided to express herself with fabric and thread. During the next 27 years she had the privilege of being included in many important national exhibitions in the fiber field, plus her work was photographed and appeared in over a dozen books. Her art has won awards and become a critical and commercial success.

Lynne believes in taking chances and allowing herself to play and have fun. In the last five years, she can classify herself as an artist who uses fabrics, threads, paper, beads, and anything else which will stimulate, inform, and transform her audience. Upon entering her studio, Lynne is ready to listen to her muses. Her studio is a world filled with endless possibilities, excitement and a "carpet" woven with a variety of beads, threads, paper and fabric snippets. This place is her sanctuary. For Lynne, making art is a daily ritual equal to breathing, eating, mothering, and loving.

Marcella Welch has been making spirit-filled dolls since childhood when as a young girl she started making dolls with her maternal grandmother. She has been making and selling her dolls professionally for over 20 years. Marcella also paints, quilts, and sculpts in various mediums, as well as creating wearable art. She believes her many talents to be God-given and her best teacher the Universe.

Marcella's work reflects her mixed cultural heritage of African and Native American Indian. Textiles and found objects from her travels to Brazil, West Africa, and South Africa often adorn her dolls, paintings, and wearable art.

Her work has been shown in major exhibitions including Uncommon Beauty in Common Objects which traveled to the Renwick Gallery of the Smithsonian Institute in Washington, D.C., the American Crafts Museum in New York, New York, and several other venues. Marcella's work is sold in several craft galleries across the United States.

Most recently, Marcella had the privilege of making a doll ornament depicting Rosa Parks for the 1999–2000 White House Christmas tree. Home and Garden Television filmed Marcella in her studio recreating the making of the Rosa Parks doll.

Visit Marcella Welch's website at www.marcellawelch.com.

Index of Gallery Artists

INDEX

ACKNOWLEDGMENTS

Thank you Barbara Evans for being a wonderful collaborative partner. Your original doll patterns laid the foundation for this book. I'm deeply indebted to you for writing the Basics chapter and supplying me with the names of so many talented doll artists to design projects and submit gallery images. I'm truly grateful for your insight, eloquence, and imagination.

Thank you Calcographer Nick for supplying the original images that accompany each sidebar. (Calcographer Nick is the alter-ego Nickie Romanuck of Medicine Hat, Alberta, Canada uses when creating her custom eraser carvings, stamping, and mail art. She enjoys the diminutive nature of working on erasers and is continually surprised by the intricacy that can be achieved.)

Thank you Susan McBride for both your exceptional talent as an art director and your good-natured soul. Throughout the project you sparkled.

Thanks to Keith and Wendy Wright for photographing the dolls with great style. Your enthusiasm, efficiency, and generous spirit make our photo shoots a dream.

Thanks to Muriel Edens for supplying flowers from your organic gardens.

In researching this book, I took part in a once-in-a-lifetime weekend. Pamela Hastings hosted a gathering of extraordinary women, all doll artists, and invited me to attend. At her lovely home in the Adirondacks, I was exposed to the spirit of cloth doll making. Kathryn Belzer, Arlinka Blair, Margi Hennen, and Tracy Stilwell joined Pamela and Skip Arthur in welcoming me into their creative circle. Getting to know these amazing artists and watching their dolls come to life was an experience I will always cherish.

I would like to thank my parents, Sara and Gerald Le Van, for their lifelong commitment to creative expression. Their example and influence guided me into this endlessly fascinating and profound world.

I'm fortunate beyond words to have Rick Morris in my life. Thank you.

This book is dedicated to my special dolls—Sara, Kate, Forrest, and Caroline.

A Note About Suppliers

Usually, the supplies you need for making the projects in Lark books can be found at your local craft supply store, discount mart, home improvement center, or retail shop relevant to the topic of the book. Occasionally, however, you may need to buy materials or tools from specialty suppliers. In order to provide you with the most up-to-date information, we have created a list of suppliers on our Web site, which we update on a regular basis. Visit us at www.larkbooks.com, click on "Craft Supply Sources," and then click on the relevant topic. You will find numerous companies listed with their web address and/or mailing address and phone number.